STUDYING NATIONAL CHARACTERS

Scholars: García, Madariaga, Tocqueville, Bennassar, Barzini, Huizinga, Triandis, Therivel

Nations: English, American, French, Spanish, German, Netherlanders, Japanese

Individualists versus Collectivists, Visitors versus Insulars

William A. Therivel

Kirk House Publishers
Minneapolis, Minnesota

STUDYING NATIONAL CHARACTERS

Scholars: García, Madariaga, Tocqueville, Bennassar, Barzini, Huizinga, Triandis, Therivel

Nations: English, American, French, Spanish, German, Netherlanders, Japanese

Individualists versus Collectivists,
Visitors versus Insulars

by William A. Therivel

Cover art: Early sixteenth century woodcut.

Library of Congress Cataloging-in-Publication Data

Therivel, William A., 1928-
  Studying national characters : scholars: Garcia, madariaga, Tocqueville, Bennassar, Barzini, Huisinga, Triandis, Therivel: nations: English, American, French, Spanish, German, Netherlanders, Japanese: individualists versus collectivists : visitors versus insulars / William A. Therivel.
    p. cm.
Includes bibliographical references and index.
ISBN-13: 978-1-933794-70-4
ISBN-10: 1-933794-70-9
1. Personality and creative ability. 2. Personality and creative ability—Cross cultural studies. I. Title.
  BF698.09.C74T484 2014
  153.4—dc23

Kirk House Publishers, P.O. Box 390759, Minneapolis, MN 55439
www.kirkhouse.com
Manufactured in the United States of America

To Brigitte and Silvia

Contents

Preface

Acknowledgment: My wife Brigitte and daughter Silvia helped me patiently with this book and it is to them that the book is dedicated.

References and footnotes follow the APA system which separates the references (at the end of the book) from the footnotes (at the bottom of each pertaining page). The separation allows for substantive footnotes that are completely devoted to expanding and clarifying thef main text. If at all possible, I would ask the reader not to skip the footnotes.

To allow the reader a direct contact with the sources most quotes are reported verbatim and not paraphrased. I use the quotes as quality bricks, or first class prefabricated sections, in no need of change on my part.

Whenever possible I have used existing translations of foreign texts; otherwise the translation is mine.

Introduction

In search of truth, enlightenment and delight, this book compares and contrasts, praises and critiques, the works of some of the best scholars on national characters:

- Carlos García on the French and Spaniards;
- Salvador de Madariaga on Englishmen, French, and Spaniards;
- Alexis de Tocqueville on the Americans;
- Bartolomé Bennassar on the Spaniards;
- Luigi Barzini on the Germans;
- Johan Huizinga on the French and Netherlanders of the Middle Ages;
- Harry Triandis on *individualism* vs. *collectivism*;
- William Therivel on *visitors* vs. *insulars.*

Four chapters are devoted to Madariaga with whose initial intuition I agree: "in the Englishman: *fair play*, in the Frenchman: *le droit*, in the Spaniard: *el honor*," but with whose subsequent elaboration—"*fair play is action*," "*le droit is intellect*," and "*el honor is passion*"—I disagree.

In the case of Barzini and Triandis, the pertaining chapters are answers to precise questions. For Barzini—from his chapter "The Mutable Germans" of his book *The Europeans* of 1983—"What is the shape of Proteus [the Germans] when caught unaware at rest?"; for Triandis—from Takeshi Hamamura, in *Personality and Social Psychology Review*—"How is it that Western societies came to become individualistic and East Asian societies collectivistic?"My answer to Hamamura makes use of what I wrote on *visitors* vs.*insulars*, and the origin of the Western *division of power* (DP), thereby causing me—with apologies—to place my chapter ahead of that on Triandis.

Similar observations apply to Huizinga, with similar apologies.

There are no separate chapters on Tocqueville and Bennassar, whom I used extensively in my critique of Madariaga: especially Tocqueville for what he said regarding the Americans.

I have kept the book small to permit, with ease, internal comparisons and contrasts.

1

García's Contrast of French and Spanish Characters

In 1616, Carlos García—an Aragonese physician who arrived in Paris between 1610 and 1614—wrote a detailed comparison and contrast (more contrast than comparison) of the character of Frenchmen and Spaniards[1], in six categories: 1. Eating and Drinking, 2. Dressing, 3. Walking, 4. Speaking, 5. Body and Soul, and 6. More on the Soul.

What García wrote is important, because later students of the Spanish character observed identical things, proof that García had a sharp eye, and that ethnopsychologies change slowly. Hereafter I report in English the most vivid and important contrasts in categories "5. Body and Soul," and (very Spanish) "6. More on the Soul."

The comparison and contrast of Frenchmen and Spaniards by García

Frenchmen are:	Spaniards are:
choleric	phlegmatic
lively	reacting slowly

---

[1] *La oposición y conjunción del los dos grandes luminares de tierra o de la antipatia natural de frances y españoles.* The first edition in Spanish is of 1617, and in French of 1618, soon followed by translations in Italian, English and German.

The above quotes, in the original Spanish, come from the 1990 synthesis by E. Temprano of the García book, as reported by Ricardo García Cárcel in his 1992 *La leyenda negra: Historia y opinion.* The English translation is mine.

merry and cheerful	melancholic and tired
daring	prudent
hasty	restrained
liberal	envious
Understand and grasp quickly and easily difficulties, but do not go beyond them, nor enter in more profound discussions.	Are slow to understand a difficulty, but once understood, grasp it tenaciously and, studying it from every angle, derive from it hundreds of consequences.
Are practical: knowing things is not enough, but they try—wherever they can—to derive from them some good or advantage. They dislike every form of idleness.	Are speculative: in their dealings they do not demand anything but contemplation, without relating them to any menial or mechanical consideration.
Devote the largest part of their scholarly studies to the law and canons, with little love for theology.	Very few study law, and nearly everybody studies theology.
Conclude their most important business dealings when they are in large company, without being disturbed by the commotion and noise.	When involved in business that requires some thinking, retire to a lonely, quiet place, and are so against company and commotion, that if a single fly comes close to their ear, while they are engrossed in their thoughts, it will prevent a decision.
Think in the present; forget all past offenses, and do not care about future benefits.	Think about both past and future; weigh their actions, with memory of the past and assumptions about the future.

In love, desires and intentions are so fickle, so changeable and chameleonic, that having given their love to somebody, they will promise it to a thousand others.	Strong, true and constant in love, adoring those they love[2], with so much fidelity, that they fear to offend the loved one even with a thought.
When favored by his lady, does not think of anything else but to inform his friends, and the whole world of his intimacy or favors.	Will try to hide this happiness from everybody, from his friends, and even from himself.
In their actions, follow only their own interest and preferences.	Love fiercely appearances and the *punto de honra*, giving more importance to general opinion than to their own interest; do not mind suffering privations and miseries, as long as this is not known.

What García wrote is fascinating, especially because it is so true, as discussed in the following chapters on the Frenchmen and Spaniards.

---

[2] For the intensity of the Spanish love, refer to Calisto's love for Melibea, in the following dialogue from *La Celestina* (of 1499) by Fernando de Rojas:

Sempronio. ¿Tú no eres christiano? (Aren't you Christian?)
Calisto. ¿Yo? Melibeo só, y Melibea adoro, y en Melibea creo, y a Melibea amo.

(I? I am Melibean, and Melibea I adore, and in Melibea I believe, and Melibea I love.)

2

Madariaga on the English, French, and Spaniards

The eminent Spanish statesman and scholar Salvador de Madariaga published a fascinating study of the character of the English, French, and Spaniards in 1929[3], titled accordingly *Englishmen, Frenchmen, Spaniards*. In the introduction he wrote:

> We shall observe in each of these three peoples a distinctive attitude which determines their natural and spontaneous reactions towards life. These reactions spring in each case from a characteristic impulse, manifesting itself in a complex psychological entity, an idea-sentiment-force peculiar to each of the three peoples, and constituting for each of them the standard of its behaviour, the key to its emotions, and the spring of its pure thoughts.

> > in the Englishman: *fair play*,
> > in the Frenchman: *le droit*,
> > in the Spaniard: *el honor*....

> **Fair play** is a term of sport. Let us note this: sport; pure action. Fair play means the perfect adaptation of the player with his team-partners but also with his adversaries. This is already wisdom. For good relations with our allies are but reason. Now wisdom is something more than reason. It is a vision of the whole, an intuition of all as one single game,

---

[3]   with a second edition in 1969.

and of opposition as a form of co-operation. Fair play implies an effacing of the individual before the team, and even of the team before the game. But this effacing does not mean annihilation. Far from it. It provides better conditions for the efficiency of the individual, since it makes his actions fit in with the actions of others in a perfect system of co-operation. This intuitive and instantaneous sense of balance between the individual and the community is the true essence of fair play.

Fair play cannot be put into formulas. It soars over all regulations, a living spirit. Elusive, yet precise; supple, yet exacting; it fits the mobile forms of life as closely as the glove the hand. As a living spirit, it manifests itself in concrete actions. It is inseparable from action, undefinable without action. It is a way of doing things. In fact, *fair play is action*....

Le droit is an idea. It is the solution which calculating Mind has contrived to the problem of the balance between the individual and the community. *Le droit* is a geometric line which, on the map of the intellect, marks the frontiers between individual liberties. While fair play fits itself to action at every moment in a perfect empirical way, *le droit* draws beforehand a scheme of rules to which it forces action to conform. While fair play occurs at the same time with action, le droit precedes it. *Le droit* is not, like fair play, a spontaneous and ever-renewed alliance between reason and nature, but a system in which nature bows to reason. And while fair play unites object and subject in the act, and, active, is neither subjective nor objective, being both simultaneously, *le droit* is coldly objective. To life's rebellions its answer is that the intellect is infallible. *Le droit is intellect.*

We saw fair play coincide with action, *le droit* precedes it; el honor follows it. In the English standard, rule and action are one; in the French standard, the rule binds action to it; in the Spanish standard, the action binds the rule to it. Nature, allied with reason in the Englishman, bowing to reason in the Frenchman, triumphs here over reason. ***El honor*** is therefore subjective, ineffable. *El honor is passion.*

The group: fair play—droit—honor leads us therefore to the group: action—intellect—passion. It would be childish to claim that each of the three peoples is, as it were, specialized so as to be entirely devoid of two-thirds of the faculties which belong to all men. Our general hypothesis goes no farther than this: that the psychological centre of gravity of each of our three peoples is placed respectively:

for the Englishman, action;

for the Frenchman, thought;

for the Spaniard, passion. (pp. 1-8)

Accordingly, action, thought and passion dominate Madariaga's book (not fair play, droit, and honor), as can be seen from its table of content:

PART ONE

   I   Action in the Man of Action
  II   Action in the Man of Thought
 III   Action in the Man of Passion
  IV   Thought in the Man of Action
   V   Thought in the Man of Thought
  VI   Thought in the Man of Passion
 VII   Passion in the Man of Action
VIII   Passion in the Man of Thought
  IX   Passion in the Man of Passion
       Conclusion

All this is fascinating, instructive and stimulating, yet in the end wrong, as discussed in the following chapters.

Madariaga was on the right track of *fair play, droit, and honor*, and should not have left them for the assumed wider world of action, thought and passion.

3

On the English, Madariaga should have stayed with the DP of *fair play*

Madariaga begins his detailed discussion of the English character with a chapter titled "Action in the Man of Action":

> THE MAN OF ACTION IN ACTION IS IN HIS ELE-MENT. We must therefore expect to find here the Englishman at his best. English people in effect excel in all aspects of action whether individual or collective.
>
> The superiority of the Englishman in action is well known. It has often been explained by the education which he gets. But, who gives the Englishman his education but the Englishman? It is not English education which explains the Englishman, but the Englishman English education. Let us watch therefore the Englishman himself. We shall see how everything in him instinctively points to action. His main preoccupation consists in being wholly at the disposal of his will at the moment when it must apply itself to the world. With this end in view, the Englishman organizes himself, disciplines himself, *controls* himself. Self-control is essentially a requirement of action. It may have evolved its philosophy and its ethics, but originally it is an instinctive and empirical tendency, the natural development of the human type specialized in action.
>
> Man is a microcosm much less unified than the outward appearance of his physical embodiment might lead us to be-

lieve. On the impact with reality it often happens that the extreme variety hidden under the apparent unity of the human being manifests itself by shattering the aims of the will, weakening the means of action, provoking internal rebellions against the decision taken. These are cases when the little people called man is under the orders of a weak Government. The Englishman sees to it that the Government of his being is solidly established. Self-control is therefore but a sound method of individual Government. In making self-control his main preoccupation, the Englishman reveals his primary tendency towards action. (pp. 12-13)

It may be so, but in this I find no link with what has been praised in the English for centuries, starting with eighteenth century *philosophes*, Voltaire in particular, as discussed by Roy Porter in *Enlightenment: Britain and the Creation of the Modern World* (2001) (p. 6):

> The *philosophes* themselves looked to England as the birthplace of the modern. Anglophiles in France, Italy and the Holy Roman Empire celebrated Britain's constitutional monarchy and freedom under the law, its open society, its prosperity and religious toleration. 'The English are the only people upon earth,' declared Voltaire in his significantly titled *Lettres philosophiques ou Lettres anglaises* (1733), the first grenade lobbed at the ancient régime,
>
>> who have been able to prescribe limits to the power of Kings by resisting them; and who, by a series of struggles, have at last established that wise Government, where the Prince is all powerful to do good, and at the same time is restrain'd from committing evil; where the Nobles are great without insolence, tho' there are no Vassals; and where the People share in the government without confusion.

Moving to the greatest of all English achievements, *Magna Carta* (1215), its virtue is not action, but DP *fair play*, from the very beginning:

John, by the grace of God, king of England, lord of Ireland, duke of Normandy and Aquitaine, and count of Anjou, to the archbishops, bishops, abbots, earls, barons, justiciars, foresters, sheriffs, stewards, servants, and to all his bailiffs and faithful subjects, greetings. Know that we, out of reverence for God and for the salvation of our soul and those of all our ancestors and heirs, for the honour of God and the exaltation of holy church, and for the reform of our realm, on the advice of our venerable fathers, Stephen, archbishop of Canterbury, primate of all England and cardinal of the holy Roman church, Henry archbishop of Dublin, William of London, Peter of Winchester, Jocelyn of Bath and Glastonbury, Hugh of Lincoln, Walter of Worcester, William of Coventry and Benedict of Rochester, bishops, of master Pandulf, subdeacon and member of the household of the lord pope, of brother Aymeric, master of the order of Knights Templar in England, and of the noble men William Marshal earl of Pembroke, William earl of Salisbury, William earl of Warenne, William earl of Arundel, Alan of Galloway constable of Scotland, Warin fitz Gerold, Peter fitz Herbert, Hubert de Burgh seneschal of Poitou, Hugh de Neville, Matthew fitz Herbert, Thomas Basset, Alan Basset, Philip de Aubeney, Robert of Ropsley, John Marshal, John fitz Hugh, and others, our faithful servants.

This long list of people who advised the King is truly fascinating in its *division of power* (DP) and *fair play* between King, Church, and Barons. In action the English are not different from say the Germans or the Japanese (very active indeed), but are very different in DP/fair play, as can be seen immediately from the beginning of the Magna Carta of the Italian Communes, the Peace of Constance of 1183, granted by Emperor Frederick Barbarossa to the members of the Lombard League:

"The mild serenity of the imperial clemency always in the habit of bestowing graces and favors on his subjects…. In accordance with the usual kindness of our grace, opening the entrails of our innate piety to the faith and homage of the Lombards….(*Pax facta*, 1976, p. 23)….We Frederick Emperor of the Romans and our son Henry King of the Romans concede, to you cities and persons of the League, the regalie and your customs as well in city and outside, also to Verona and its castle, to suburbs and other cities, land and persons of the League, in perpetuity" (*Pax facta*, p. 23).

In this there is no hint of power sharing, no hint of fair play. The Emperor is alone in his knowledge, no need of advice, alone in acting and granting.

Back to Magna Carta: its first article speaks of the liberties of the Church, of how King and Church will play fair:

[1] In the first place have granted to God, and by this our present charter confirmed for us and our heirs for ever that the English church shall be free, and shall have its rights undiminished and its liberties unimpaired; and it is our will that it be thus observed; which is evident from the fact that, before the quarrel between us and our barons began, we willingly and spontaneously granted and by our charter confirmed the freedom of elections which is reckoned most important and very essential to the English church, and obtained confirmation of it from the lord pope Innocent III; the which we will observe and we wish our heirs to observe it in good faith forever. We have also granted to all free men of our kingdom, for ourselves and our heirs forever, all the liberties written below, to be had and held by them and their heirs of us and our heirs.

"The English church shall be free, and shall have its rights undiminished and its liberties unimpaired"! and "We have also granted to all free men of our kingdom, for ourselves and our heirs forever, all the liberties written below, to be had and held by them and their heirs of us and our heirs"! These are great DP statements. They are *fair play* of the first order, in which each element of society has power and interacts with the others with fairness.

And then we have the fair play of individual articles, as for instance:

[7] A widow shall have her marriage portion and inheritance forthwith and without difficulty after the death of her husband; nor shall she pay anything to have her dower or her marriage portion or the inheritance which she and her husband held on the day of her husband's death; and she may remain in her husband's house for forty days after his death, within which time her dower shall be assigned to her.

[8] No widow should be forced to marry so long as she wishes to live without a husband, provided that she gives security not to marry without our consent if she holds of us, or without the consent of her lord of whom she holds, if she holds of another.

[9] Neither we nor our bailiffs will seize for any debt any land or rent, so long as the chattels of the debtor are sufficient to repay the debt.

[13] And the city of London shall have all its ancient liberties and free customs as well by land as by water. Furthermore, we will and grant that all other cities, boroughs, towns, and parts shall have all their liberties and free customs.

More than five hundred years after the signing of Magna Carta we have that other "Anglo Charter" rooted in fair play: The 1776 *Declaration of Independence* of the United States of America, starting with:

When in the Course of human events, it becomes necessary for one people to dissolve the political bands which have connected them with another, and to assume among the powers of the earth, the separate and equal station to which the Laws of Nature and of Nature's God entitle them, a decent respect to the opinions of mankind requires that they should declare the causes which impel them to the separation.— We hold these truths to be self-evident, that all men are created equal, that they are endowed by their Creator with certain unalienable Rights, that among these are Life, Liberty and the pursuit of Happiness.— That to secure these rights, Governments are instituted among Men, deriving their just powers from the consent of the governed.

These pronouncements are pure fair play (and some action). The opposite affirmation would be unfair, yet equal in action.

Sixty years later,Tocqueville praises the American character in his Democracy in America of 1835-40:

> Americans of all ages, all conditions, and all dispositions constantly form association. They have not only commercial and manufacturing companies, in which all take part, but associations of a thousand other kinds, religious, moral, serious, futile, general or restricted, enormous or diminutive. The Americans make associations to give entertainments, to found seminaries, to build inns, to construct churches, to diffuse books, to send missionaries to the antipodes, in this manner they found hospitals, prisons, and schools. If it is proposed to inculcate some truth or to foster some feeling by the encouragement of a great example, they form a society. Wherever at the head of some new undertaking you see the government in France, or a man of rank in England, in the United States you will be sure to find an association.
>
> I met with several kinds of associations in America of which I confess I had no previous notion; and I have often admired the extreme skill with which the inhabitants of the United States succeed in proposing a common object for the exertions of a great many men and in inducing them voluntarily to pursue it....
>
> Nothing, in my opinion, is more deserving of our attention than the intellectual and moral associations of America. (1835-40/1987, pp. 106, 109)

Equally rooted, more in fair play than in action, is Toqueville's praise of "How the American views the Equality of the Sexes":

> I think that the same social impetus which brings nearer to the same level [fair play] father and son, master and servant, and generally every inferior to every superior does raise the status of women and should make them more and more nearly equal to men....In the United States men seldom compliment women, but they daily show how much they esteem them.
>
> Americans constantly display complete confidence in their spouses' judgment and deep respect for their freedom.

They hold that woman's mind is just as capable as man's of discovering the naked truth, and her heart as firm to face it. They have never sought to place her virtue, any more than his, under the protection of prejudice, ignorance, or fear.

For my part, I have no hesitation in saying that although the American woman never leaves her domestic sphere and is in some respects very dependent within it, nowhere does she enjoy a higher station. And now that I come near the end of this book in which I have recorded so many considerable achievements of the Americans, if anyone asks me what I think the chief cause of the extraordinary prosperity and growing power of this nation, I should answer that it is due to the superiority of their women. (1835-40/1988, pp. 600-03)

Once more, Madariaga was correct in seeing fair play as the character differentiating the English [and the Americans] from say the French and the Spaniards, but mistaken in translating fair play with action.

4

On the French, Madariaga should have stayed with *droit*

1. Barzini first, then García and Madariaga

In *The Quarrelsome French*, the fourth part of Barzini's book on the Europeans, he makes a key observation:

> Perhaps it is their very innate restlessness, love of strife, and some disorder that made it necessary from the beginning to try to weave around them one of the most intricate webs of codes, laws, regulations, and norms in the world, in an effort to foresee and control every possible circumstance and contingency of life. (1983, p. 139).

"Codes, laws, regulations, and norms," in other words "*droit*" (the law), that same *droit* highlighted by Carlos García:

> *La mayor parte de los entendimientos franceses se dan al estudio de las leyes y canones, y muy poco aman la teologia*; (The largest part of the French understanding is devoted to the study of the laws and canons, with little love for theology);

and by Salvador de Madariaga:

> *Le droit* is not, like fair play, a spontaneous and ever-renewed alliance between reason and nature, but a system in which nature bows to reason... *Le droit* is coldly objective. To life's rebellions its answer is that the intellect is infallible. *Le droit is intellect*. (ib., p. 5)

Yet, that *droit which is intellect*, is also, and very much so, the intellect of the legislators, of those in power who want their rule to be obeyed. All *droit* is intellect, but not all intellect is *droit* (as noted by García above), therefore in the study of the French character we cannot leave *droit* for thought in general. On the contrary we must pay close attention to the very French legalistic/rhetorical form of thinking; a form of thinking that goes back to the centuries of Roman domination of Gaul.

2. France's Roman roots

Gaul was Rome's best pupil... The Merovingians and Carolingians, barbarians as they still were, had imitated the laws of Rome with touching zeal — Edouard Driault (quoted by Geyl, 1949, p. 342, when discussing Driault's *The Roman Education of France*).

More than any other part of the Roman empire, France remained romanized, whereas the whole of north Africa and Spain, as well as the Middle East, were swept away by the Arabs. Greece reverted to Hellenism during the later years of the Byzantine empire, and then it too was swept away by Islamic conquerors. Italy could have remained as romanized as France had it not been for the destructions brought about by the attempts of the Byzantine empire to reconquer it.

Italy:

It took the Byzantines nearly two decades to destroy Ostrogothic resistance. The Gothic war [ca. 535-553], as it has been called, ruined Italy economically. Italy suffered a devastating blow from which it did not recover until the tenth century. By the middle of the sixth century a noticeable deurbanization had taken place; the great cities, such as Rome, Naples, and Milan had suffered catastrophic loss of population,... The Gothic war is the decisive point in the economic and social history of early medieval Italy, a far more important break than the Germanic invasions of the fifth century. Italy declined rapidly from her traditional position as the cultural and economic leader of Europe. (Cantor, 1993, p. 128)

France:

In contrast to Theoderic's brilliant and doomed political structure in Italy, Clovis's kingdom from the beginning experienced a much more thorough mixture of Frankish and Roman traditions. Moreover, Gaul and Germany were simply too peripheral to Byzantine concerns to attract more than the cursory interest of Justinian and his successors. Thus the Franks were left to work out the implications of their successes in relative peace.... [Particularly] important for the establishment of continuity and effectiveness was the dual Roman heritage of both conquerors and conquered.... Not only did Latin letters and language continue to be cultivated and vulgar Roman law continue to order people's lives, but Roman fiscal and agricultural structures, the network of Roman roads, towns, and commercial systems, although greatly privatized, had nevertheless survived without serious interruptions.... The Franks themselves were likewise deeply Romanized.... The Franks of Clovis's time were accustomed to Roman traditions of law. They were equally accustomed, or soon made themselves so, to the use of Roman administration. (Geary, 1988, pp. 89-92)

Many Franks "wanted to be Gallo Roman, though in actual fact they became French.... The administrative shape of Frankish Gaul is sub-Roman, and it uses the old Latin terms ... held together, however loosely, by common experience of the forms of Roman rule, most particularly as expressed by Roman Law" (Wallace-Hadrill, 1957, p. 36).

Later, during the Renaissance, the French reverted to the classical world like ducks to water: "The centuries of France's primary allegiance to form [a few decades before 1500 to around 1750] have as their base the civilization and culture of classical antiquity.... [Boileau modelled his *Art poétique* of 1674] after that of a most sophisticated and correct Roman, Quintus Horatius Flaccus. Boileau was himself a fine example in modern Gaul, of Roman urbanity" (Wiley, 1967, pp. 9, 14).

Sadly, along with the adoption of the Roman legal system, came the equally Roman tendency toward imperialism. The Merovingian kings were already in the process of establishing an imperial absolutism according to the Roman precedent: "The king was supreme head of the armies.... He chose ministers and officers as he pleased, and enriched his treasury by taking bribes for an appointment. *He held the Church under control, convening episcopal councils and interfering with the elections to vacant sees.* He was above justice, and had arbitrary power of life and death. He could change old laws and make new ones" (Dalton, 1927, p. 193; my italics).

In the words of Lord Acton: "Roman Gaul had so thoroughly adopted the ideas of absolute authority and undistinguished equality during the five centuries between Caesar and Clovis, that the people could never be reconciled to the new [feudal] system. Feudalism remained a foreign importation, and the feudal aristocracy an alien race, *and the common people of France sought protection against both in the Roman jurisprudence and the power of the crown.*" (1862/1972, p. 150; my italics,in order to highlight the royal unity of power [UP] over State and Church).

Yet, that protection became too much with the neo-Roman Napoleonic Code Civil.

3. Colbert and the nostalgia for Ancient Rome

Inés Murat—in the section titled "The state as dispenser of justice" in her biography of Colbert—wrote that, during the *Grand Siècle* (1610-1715), "An intense need for unification, order, and simplicity went hand in hand with a very fashionable nostalgia for Ancient Rome.... [Colbert] had researchers find for him the great principles of Roman law. He had a sort of sentimental conception of Augustan Rome—powerful, deriving its strength from its unity and the clarity of its administration.... The king, God's delegate, consecrated by the Church, was the natural protector of the people and the supreme judge (1984, pp. 91-2).

The next step—similar to that taken by Emperor Justinian—was to collate all edicts into a single body. This was so well done that it was "used by the Revolution, a century later.... The ordinance for commerce, dating from 1673, fixed French commerce of an extended period. The creator of the Napoleonic Code would borrow many of its provisions and would even copy entire passages from it" (ib. p. 242). Also, Colbert's "civil ordinance of 1667 served as model for the civil procedure in the Napoleonic Code" (ib., p. 280).

4. The Napoleonic *Droit* of 1804

The Code Civil of 1804 has been described as an effort 'to consolidate the achievement of the Revolution, *to reconcile the customary law with the Roman law*, and to effect a smooth transition from past to the present'" (Yianopoulos, 1973, p. 11, my italics).

The Code Civil was drafted as a model for good citizens, and is based on obedience to the state. Equality is seen as equality before the state apparatus, and freedom is seen as the state's ability to regulate and adjust conflicting interests" (Gramont, 1969, p. 204).

The neo-Roman aspects of the Napoleonic Code Civil of 1804 are particularly evident in a comparison of the Anglo-American common law with the French civil law: "*A reception of Roman law, such as had developed on the Continent, was prevented in England.* At the same time a strong connection was established between the principles of constitutionalism and individual freedom, a*nd the common law as the legal system of freedom,in contrast to the civil law, in which the state is exalted over the individual.* This image gained additional support from the fact that free political institutions were developed earlier and have been maintained more firmly in countries of the common law than in countries of the civil law" (Rheinstein & Glendon, 1993, p. 920; my italics).

5. Rhetoric, that key tool of *Droit*

Ernest Renan called rhetoric "*The French ailment,* which is the need to perorate, the tendency to make everything into rhetoric, nurtured by the University's obstinacy in respecting nothing but style and talent" (1859; quoted by Peyrefitte, 1976/1981, p. vii). Earlier, this tendency had been called "The Gallic ailment," when Cato was saying that "The Gauls have two passions: to fight, and to talk" (quoted by Funck-Brentano, 1925, p. 58).

More to the point: "Rome exploited a feature of the Gallic character which Caesar had earlier noted and exploited, namely a strong taste for gatherings and conferences (no doubt stimulated by, and itself stimulating, the famous Gallic love of rhetoric)" (Drinkwater, 1983, p. 111). In turn, this passion to talk should have greatly facilitated the acquisition and mastery of Roman rhetoric, and Roman *droit*.

6. Rhetoric for the sake of rhetoric

It seems to me an acknowledged fact [wrote Madame de Staël in 1810], that Paris is, of all cities in the world, that in which the spirit and taste for conversation are most generally diffused; and that disorder, which they call the mal du pays, that undefinable longing for our native land, which exists independently even of the friends we have left behind there, applies particularly to the pleasure of conversation which Frenchmen find nowhere else in the same degree as at home....The necessity of conversation is felt by all classes of people in France: speech is not there, as elsewhere, merely the means of communicating from one to another ideas, sentiments, and transactions; but it is an instrument on which they are fond of playing, and which animates the spirits, like music among some people, and strong liquors among others.

That sort of pleasure, which is produced by an animated conversation, does not precisely depend on the nature of that conversation; the idea and knowledge [pace Madariaga on the priority of thought] which it develops do not form its principal interest; it is a certain manner of acting upon one another, of giving mutual and instantaneous delight, of speaking the moment one thinks, of acquiring immediate self-enjoyment, of receiving applause without labor, of displaying the understanding in all its shades by accent, gesture, look, of eliciting, in short, at will, the electric sparks, which relieve some of the excess of their vivacity, and serve to awaken others out of a state of painful apathy.

Nothing is more foreign to this talent than the character and disposition of the German intellect; they require in all things a serious result. (1810/1887, pp. 77-78)

7. The very best in French rhetoric:La Fontaine's Le Corbeau et le Renard

Le Corbeau et le Renard

Maître corbeau, sur un arbre perché,
Tenait en son bec un fromage.
Maître renard, par l'odeur alléché,
Lui tint à peu près ce langage:
    "Eh! bonjour, Monsieur du Corbeau.
    Que vous êtes joli! que vous me semblez beau!
    Sans mentir, si votre ramage
    Se rapporte à votre plumage,
    Vous êtes le phénix des hôtes de ces bois."
A ces mots le corbeau ne se sent pas de joie;
Et pour montrer sa belle voix,
Il ouvre un large bec, laisse tomber sa proie.
Le renard s'en saisit, et dit:
    "Mon bon monsieur,
    Apprenez que tout flatteur
    Vit aux dépens de celui qui l'écoute:
    Cette leçon vaut bien un fromage, sans doute."
Le corbeau, honteux et confu,
Jura, mais un peu tard, qu'on ne l'y prendrait plus.

The Crow and the Fox

Master Crow, perched in a tree, was holding a piece of cheese in his beak;

Master Fox, attracted by the smell, addressed him so:

"Oh, good day to you, Lord Crow! How beautiful you are! How fine and fair!

In truth, if your singing is as wonderful as your plumage, you are the phoenix of the inhabitants of this forest."

The crow, beside himself with joy and pride, opened his beak to show his beautiful voice, and dropped the cheese. The fox seized it, and said:

"My good Sir, do learn that every flatterer thrives at the cost of those who listen to him:

This lesson, no doubt, is worth a cheese."

The crow, shamefaced and flustered, swore, too late, that he would never be fooled again.

Le Corbeau et le Renard is a concentric spider web of rhetoric and logic from which the Crow is unable to escape. First he is told: "Oh, good day to you, Lord Crow! How beautiful you are! How fine and fair!" a statement of facts, rhetorically vivid, and adroitly introduced by that flattering salute of "Good day to you, Lord Crow!" Then comes a perfect piece of logical derivation, a first-class syllogism: "In truth, if your singing is as wonderful as your plumage, you are the phoenix of the inhabitants of this forest."

Not having refused either salutation or compliment, the Crow is trapped.

But was it really for the cheese? Given that it was a French *renard*, and not an English fox or Spanish zorro, one may harbor the suspicion that the real pleasure of the renard does not consist in the loot, in the cheese, but in the sermon he can preach to the *corbeau*: in showing how rhetorically smart he is. That was the real victory.

And the Crow is fooled also for the lack of that other type of mistrust, less logical, not rhetorical, but pragmatic, as proclaimed by Willard Duncan Vandiver in 1899:

> I come from a state that raises corn and cotton and cockleburs and Democrats, and frothy eloquence neither convinces nor satisfies me. I am from Missouri. You have got to show me.

Here, Vandiver stressed first the material activities of his state: raising corn, cotton, and cockleburs (a coarse weed bearing closed prickly seedcases); then, he refused rhetoric, rhetorical logic, and theory; and finally he asked for facts, for empirical evidence.

The French people cannot operate this way, because each of them loves his own rhetoric, his formalism, his logic, his theories, his plans. If he refuses them in others, he automatically denies his own chance to display his own rhetoric, formalism, logic, theories and plans. He cannot escape the game: he is the willing, and enthusiastic, participant in a great baroque game which he wants to win, not to eliminate. Therefore, his mistrust is different, non-Missourian, based on listening carefully to detect any fallacy in the logic, any rhetorical distortion. His first line of defense consists in the lesson given by the fox: "My good Sir, do learn that every flatterer thrives at the cost of those who listen to him: This lesson, no doubt, is worth a cheese." Then, his second defense will be in reading and re-reading every piece of paper, be it legislation, contract, or love-letter: somebody is there to get him, and he must discover it; while still enjoying the flattery inherent in every piece of rhetoric.

Then, striving for perfection, the French will upgrade their mistrust to the glory of a logical system. Theirs will not be plain, vulgar, banausic, empirical or applied mistrust but a whole *Discours de la méthode* in which mistrust acquires a universal scope. It becomes the *De omnibus dubitandum* → *De omnibus dubio* → *Dubito ergo sum* → *Cogito ergo sum: "Je me méfie, donc je suis."*[4]

8. Madariaga also spoke of the French mistrust, but he tied it to thought and not to *droit* (the suspected *droit* of the state)

As noted by Madariaga:

There is a distinction, as essential as evident, between French order and English spontaneous organization. English spontaneous organization is free, instinctive, vital, omnipresent, natural, simultaneous with action, unwritten. French order is official. Imposed from above though accepted below, intellectual, artificial, regulated, preceding action by a complicated system of written laws which aim at foreseeing all possible cases. The intellectualistic tendency gets hold of the field of action, limits and defines it, and throws over it a network of principles to which all future action most conform. This network of principles is le droit. These principles of course remain, in their perfect regularity, too far from the irregularities of life. In order to hold to things in action more closely, the intellectual inserts within the network of *le droit* another network finer still: *les règlements*.

We are therefore in the realm of *les règlements* dictated by foresight and inspired by distrust. While in England the anonymous citizen is supposed to be innocent until the contrary be proved, in France the anonymous citizen is considered

---

[4]   "Doubt everything → I doubt everything → I doubt therefore I am→ I think therefore I am → I am suspicious therefore I am."

as a hypothetical being in whom all evil intentions conspire
and against whose Machiavellian plans the State must be
ever on guard. We are no longer in that English atmosphere
of peace and co-operation between all citizens, grouped in
a healthy and active collective being, working without co-
ercion for a common aim, but on the contrary, in a kind of
war atmosphere in which officials, solidly entrenched behind
their desks, assiduously prepare battle plans against X with all
the military genius of real Napoleons. French bureaucracy is
therefore but the natural consequence in the collective world
of the feature which we consider as fundamental in French
psychology, i.e. the predominance of intellectual standards.
(ib., pp. 32-33)

However the culprit is not the predominance of intellectual standards, but the predominance of the *unity of power,* be it of Louis XIV
(L'état c'est moi)[5], Napoleon I[6] and III, or De Gaulle, in a "society
in which mistrust—a lack of confidence—seems dominant. The individual depends on various hierarchies for all the actions of his life.
They command, judge him, indicate what he must do because they
know better than he where his happiness lies. Authority is exercised

[5] "But the King's most vicious method of securing information was opening letters.
Through their ignorance and imprudence, a great many people continued to provide him
with information for years, until the system was exposed. That is why the Pajots and the
Rouilles, who were responsible for the postal service, were so respected they could never
be removed, or even promoted. The cause long remained a mystery, and they amassed
enormous fortunes at the expense of the public and the King. The skill and efficiency of
the letter-opening operation defies the imagination. The postmasters and the postmaster
general sent the King extracts of all the letters that could interest him, and copies of entire
letters when the content or the rank of the sender warranted it. It took so little to condemn
someone that those in charge of the postal system, from chiefs to clerks, were able to
accuse whomever they wanted. They did not even have to rely on forgeries or prolonged
investigations; one word of contempt for the King or his government, one jeer taken out of
context and plausibly presented, sufficed to condemn without appeal or inquiry, and this
means was always at their fingertips. The number of people who were rightly or wrongly
condemned is inconceivable. The King's secret was never discovered, and nothing ever cost
him less than to conceal it with profound silence." (Duc de Saint-Simon, 1694-1723/1990,
pp. 146-47). (*)

(*) See *Le Cabinet Noir* (1950) by Eugène Vaillé, Conservateur du Musée Postal

[6] *"Pourtant, en dernière analyse, Napoléon, ne croyait qu'à la force. 'On ne gouverne
qu'avec des éperons et des bottes.'"* (Maurois, 1964, p. 76). ("In the last analysis, Napoleon
believed only in force.'One rules only with spurs and boots.')

from the top down. The leader's character is sacred" (Peyrefitte, 1981, p. 24)

Returning to Madariaga:

The Administration is the strongest force working for uniformity and centralization in France. It possesses a marvelous capacity for absorbing public functions which in other countries, such as England, remain outside the State...But what of the people? The people are too intelligent really to believe in liberty; too calculating to compromise on the subject of equality; too busy with their own affairs to care to take over those of the community, and too mistrustful to allow the community, i.e. the State, to take too much care of their own....

The very opposition which seems to exist between the tendency to prevision in the Frenchman in action, and the dislike of all intellectual prevision which is one of the typical characteristics of English thought, is but another form of this symmetry: *the Frenchman foresees because he mistrusts life; the Englishman refuses to foresee because he mistrusts thought.* (ib., pp. 153-4, 111)

"*The Frenchman foresees because he mistrusts life*" is very true. Why does he mistrust life? Because of his powerful thinking, or rather because he is imprisoned by droit? Imprisoned by the droit of the state? By a state permeated with Roman thinking, Roman laws, Roman rhetoric?

5

On the Spaniards, Madariaga should have stayed with *honor* (more correctly *honra*)

1. As studied by Madariaga

On Spain, Madariaga would have been clearer if he had spoken of *la honra*, and not of *el honor*, because what really differentiates Spain from all other Western countries is her emphasis, not on an internal or intrinsic honor, but on a communal *honra* strongly dependent on public opinion which determines who has *honra* or not, who had it and lost it, as noted before by Carlos García:

> The Spaniards love fiercely the appearances and the *punto de honra*, giving more importance to the general opinion than to their own interest; thus they do not mind suffering all kinds of poor conditions and miseries, as long as this is not known.

2. Honor, *honra*, and the UP power of public opinion

Starting with a dictionary: *Punto de honra or pundonor is the "Estado en que, según la común opinión, consiste la honra o crédito de uno"*. [The *pundonor* is the condition which determines, according to the general opinion, the honor or credit of a person.]

Both the Spanish words *honor* and *honra* derive from the Latin honor, but while the Spanish *honor* is identical to the Latin *honor,* and both reflect an internal, or intrinsic condition, the Spanish honra (at the base of the *pundonor*), instead, stems more specifically from the Latin verb *honorar* which reflects what others do, or do not do, in honoring a given person.

Honra and *pundonor* bring others and their opinion into play the others, their opinion, far more than *honor*. Correspondingly, two of the great theatrical works of Calderón de la Barca are titled *El médico de su honra* (The surgeon of his *honra*) and *El pintor de su deshonra* (The painter of his *dishonra*), in which both the surgeon and the painter were primarily concerned with public opinion.

Also, as observed by Marcelin Defourneaux in his the *Daily Life in Spain in the Golden Age* [1550-1650]:

No man is entirely the master of his honour [honra], and the theatre of the Golden Age—like the code of the Partidas four centuries before—keeps reminding us that honour can always be tarnished by others. Thus the dictum of Lope de Vega:

> No man attains to honour by himself,
> For it is the gift of other men.
> A virtuous and well-deserving man
> Need not attain to honour: so it is thus
> That honour stems from others, not oneself.

Moreover, honour having an absolute value in public opinion, mere suspicion even though unjustified can bring upon a man an inexorable punishment. (1966/1979, p. 33-4)

[For Bennassar] If there was one passion capable of defining the conduct of the Spanish people, [wrote Bennassar] it was the passion of honor. Rarely have such diverse sources been in such perfect accord on this point[7] ....What, then, is honor? To begin with, it is a particular form of pride, with the

---

[7]   One of these sources was probably the *hidalgo,* who employed—without pay or food—Lazarillo de Tormes:
Eres mochacho, y no sientes las cosas de la honra, en que el día de hoy está todo el caudal de los hombres de bien. (Anon. 1554/1982, p. 148)(*)
[You are just a boy, and do not understand what is honra, which, in our times, constitutes all the fortune of the honest men.]

(*) Published anonymously because of its heretical content and open criticism of the Catholic Church.

result that foreign writers have sometimes confused the two. This special form of pride demanded the transcendence of the individual at the cost of one's life, if necessary. This means that the display of honor is almost always public; it requires witnesses. It is by virtue of its public character that honor becomes a socialized value based on reputation and transcends the individual. Accordingly, a man can lose his or her honor without having acted dishonorably.... But honor was already becoming the hostage of reputation. Its social significance surpassed its individual significance, and it was therefore condemned to follow the evolution of Spanish society. And as that society shriveled, ossified, codified its prohibitions, the conception of honor changed together with the society; it became constraining, wholly dependent on public opinion. Mateo Aleman, the author of Guzman de Alfarache, documents this when he has his hero say: 'What a burden is this burden of honor.... How difficult it is to acquire and preserve; how easy to lose merely on account of the common opinion" (1979, p. 213, 215, 223-4).

Looking specifically at the drawbacks of *pundonor* Bennassar wrote:

Simultaneously, *pundonor* began to place under interdict certain kinds of labor, the "mechanical" activities in general.... The enlightened Gonzalez de Cellorigo lamented that chivalric honor had gone astray by rejecting labor, and sought to prove that the practice of agriculture or commerce had never entailed the loss of honor. Despite the efforts of Cellorigo and other *arbitristas*, the prejudice against labor grew stronger throughout the seventeenth century and continued down to the nineteenth century. It was this distorted *pundonor* that made Larra's protagonist in *El Casarse pronto y mal* refuse every offer of employment. (ib. p. 230)

"So great is the love of ease, so far advanced Spain's perdition," wrote Luis Ortiz in a memorialto King Philip II [r. 1556-98], "that none, whatever his state or condition, will hear of working at any craft or business, but must go to the University of Salamanca, or to the Italian wars or the Indies, or became a notary public or attorney, all to the ruin of the commonwealth." (ib. p. ix)

Francisco Gómes de Quevedo [1580-1645] described the dismal social consequences of pundonor: "A poor gentleman is starving, he has nothing to wear, his closes are tattered and patched, perhaps he becomes a thief; yet he does not ask for anything because he says he has honor, nor does he want to serve because he says it is dishonorable" (Keen, 1979, pp. ix, x).

For centuries Spain was a land of chronic violence. Contained, indeed successfully repressed, in the age of the Catholic Sovereigns, then by Charles V and Philip II by judicial institutions of high quality, it surged up again from the seventeenth to the nineteenth century. *I am not suggesting that the Hispanic conception of honor was responsible for all or even for the majority of the acts of violence of this period, but it certainly encouraged them.*(Bennassar, 1979, p. 233, my italics)

3. Similar observations on the Arabs

Social pressure in Arab society is tremendous. Public opinion is the main force that judges, praises or condemns the behavior of the individual; it is the immediate as well as the ultimate power for controlling his actions. It leaves him with little choice for directing his own conduct. Since the internal freedom he enjoys is very slight, he is constantly watching for the opinions of his community. One of the basic problems of life in Arab society is the fear of each other's opinion.

The object of fear is personified in society. As it curbs his actions, threatens him with constant shame, and often misjudges his acts, the Arab feels society to be his worst enemy. Rarely does he receive credit for his good deeds, but if he errs, the whip of society is always at hand. Social control in Arab society is based largely on shaming; hence it depends on primary and close groups in which everyone knows everyone else's acts. (Hamady, 1960, pp. 34-5)

Honor in the Arab world is a generic concept which embraces many different forms. To mention only a few: there is the kind of honor a man derives from his virility as manifested in having numerous sons;... It is honorable to exhibit a strong sense of kin group adherence.... Cost what it may, one must defend one's public image.... All these different kinds of honor, clearly distinguished in Arab life and operative at various times and on various occasions, interlock to surround the Arab ego like a coat of armor. The smallest chink in this armor can threaten to loosen al the loops and rings, and must therefore be repaired immediately and with determination. (Patai, 1983, p. 91, my italics).

In *The Closed Circle: An Interpretation of the Arabs*, David Pryce-Jones, wrote that:

Honor is what makes life worthwhile: shame is a living death not to be endured, requiring that it be avenged.... Honor and its recognition set up the strongest patterns of conduct, in a hierarchy of deference and respect....By definition, honor and shame involve publicity. There can be no honor without show and even swagger. Display has priority over reticence and self-control. Whoever judges that honor is due to him must demand it; he must brook no interference or delay in his affairs. (1989, pp. 35-6, 40)

4. *Honra* and hyperindividualism

Paradoxically at first, the pressure of common opinion, aimed at keeping people in the fold and working for the common good, fostered in Spain the development of an exacerbated proud individualism prone to all kinds of violence at the mere appearance of an offense to his honra. This was a direct consequence of the Reconquista that demanded military valor at any moment, the alternative being a defeat, and a return of the Muslims. Pride provided the necessary adrenalin. The *hidalgo* had to be brave, and proud. His strong sense of *honra* was needed by society.

However, what was a great plus in those times, became a handicap later, when a more harmonious society was based on work and not on war anymore. Being brave and proud, and having a strong sense of honra, is of little use in agriculture, commerce, industry, education, social and cultural development.

Later, the emphasis would be on pride without deeds: pride in one's untouched *honra*; a pride decried by Sánchez-Albornoz when he spoke of: "*la sinfonía del orgullo hispano... el yo explosivo de los españoles... el hiperindividualismo hispano*" [the symphony of hispanic pride/haughtiness... the explosive I of the Spaniards... the Spanish hyperindividualism]. (1991, pp. 1227, 1339).

Bennassar, aptly summarized the former positive and subsequently negative aspect of honor:

> The persistence of honor as a national passion, as a powerful motivating force, does not at all mean that its nature and effects remained all the same over the centuries. Defined during the Reconquest, honor first appeared as a positive value.... [Later] honor was becoming the hostage of reputation [and the source of much violence]. (p. 223)

Honor was equally hostage of reputation during the Reconquest. Only that, in those time, a reputation of honor (specifically of courage in front of the enemy) had a social purpose: it was a valid script. Despite the passage of time, the script remained the same but in a different context it became negative, especially when adopted—as touchy *pundonor*—by larger sections of the population.

The next question is why the touchy purposeless pundonor continued for so long. Part of the answer comes from Sánchez-Albornoz who stressed how recent the Reconquest (712-1492) is in comparison with the great barbarian migrations of the 4th, 5th, and 6th centuries which shaped the West; even the Norman invasion of England, dates from as far back as 1077. Indeed, ethnoscripts change very slowly. But probably the unity of power of the Spanish kings which prevented a change which would have been difficult to control, was even more important in retaining pundonor. Some change occured, but toward an insular mentality and not toward a visitor one, as discussed in chapter 10.

Like Bennassar, Sánchez-Albornoz is in a quandary: he points to a positive Spanish epoch (Phase 1), when pride and individualism were constructive, but he also identifies its destructive evolution (Phase 2).

On Phase 1, he wrote that:

> This Spanish hyperindividualism is not of today nor of yesterday, but of always.... It is linked with the Iberic pride and passion. Pride and passion are the essential leaven (yeast) of every individualism. Without pride and passion it is not possible to put the springs of the human person under tension.... The individualism, by saving us from the servitude of the collective, by making us original and unique, liberate us from the torture that people suffer when feeling crushed by the yoke of social tyranny. (1991, pp. 705-7)

But, then, for Phase 2 he wrote:

> Only his spiritual lethargy and his excess of individualism—each cared only for his liberty not that of everybody—can explain the failure,.... Paraphrasing the well known words of Francis I, after the battle of Pavia, one could say that we have lost all save our honor and arrogance. (ib., pp. 1343, 1375)

5. More on *honra* and hyperindividualism

At the beginning of his book on Las Casas, Lewis Hanke wrote that "The phrase 'My country, right or wrong!' could never have been struck off by a Spaniard. One of those popular sayings which reveal some of the basic wisdom of the Spanish character puts it this way:

> *Si habla bien de Inglaterra, es inglés,*
> *Si habla mal de Alemania, es francés,*
> *Si habla mal de España, es español.*

> Who speaks well of England, is an Englishman,
> Who speaks ill of Germany, is a Frenchman,
> Who speaks ill of Spain, is a Spaniard."(1951, p. 1).

However, there is a praise of Spain, which few Englishmen would ever proffer for England. In *Ser español* of 1987, Marías reports with admiration how Ortega, in a paper of 1910, said with *"pocas palabras modestas y ambiciosas: 'Queremos la interpretación española del mundo'* [In a few modest and ambitious words, 'We seek the Spanish interpretation of the world'] (p. 214).

As strong as this demand was, it was not new: in 1906, Unamuno had written a whole essay titled *"Sobre la europeización"* [On the Europeization] in which he said:

> I have the profound conviction that the true and meaningful Europeization of Spain, i.e. our digestion of that part of the European spirit which can become our spirit, will not begin until we can impose ourselves on the European spiritual order, until we manage to have Europe accept our, the genuine our, in exchange of his, until we will manage to hispanisize Europe. (1951, p. 918).

6. Ortega y Gasset's contrast of French and Spaniards: In France life is scrupulous enjoyment, in Spain: Life is a universal toothache

In *Espiritu de la letra* (1927), Ortega y Gasset raised an important question:

> Why is France the country in which the most memoirs have been written, always; and Spain is the country of the fewest?
>
> The memoirs are a symptom of the pleasure of life. Not only did one live it well, but enjoys reviewing it.... It is applauding one's life before its end. The memoirs are a delectatio morosa [a scrupulous enjoyment] in the great sin of living.... The temper of the Spaniards is exactly the opposite. The scarcity of memoirs and novels does not surprise if we remember that the Spaniard feels life like a universal toothache [*un universal dolor de muelas*]. (pp. 123, 125)

Why? The answer has much to do with geography: economic geography (percent of cultivable land, amount of rain, number of powerful rivers, etc.,) favoring France; and historical geography equally favoring France. On this last, Spain was conquered by Arab/ Muslim armies in 711-712 A.D. Large sections of Spain remained under Muslim domination, and much of the population converted to the faith of Muhammad, spoke Arabic, and adopted many Arab customs and scripts. The domination was long: only in 1085 could the Christians reconquer Toledo, Cordoba as late as 1236, Seville in 1248, and Granada in 1492.

France, instead, was spared by the victory over Muslim invaders from Spain at Poitiers—260 miles north of the Pyrenees—by Charles Martel, in 732.

Spain suffered from being so near to Muslim North-Africa. France was saved by distance and the protective barrier of the Pyrenees.

One sad consequence of the Arab invasion and long centuries of war against Muslim armies to achieve the *Reconquista*, was the adoption of a strict sense of honor, in reality of honra.

7. Envy

Madariaga would also have made a stronger argument by linking envy to honor/honrarather than to passion:

> The Spaniard, in spite of many misconceptions, is not theatrical, but dramatic. He conceives life as a drama and judges things and people from the view of a spectator. This fact is full of political consequences... it explains why the Spanish people usually suffers from envy, which is, so to say, its specific defect. (ib., p. 44)

Is envy a specific Spanish defect?

Yes, for Carlos Garcia who wrote, as early as 1616:"The Spaniards: Very envious. The French: Very liberal in disposing generously of their possessions".

More recent observers wrote:
> The fact that the most generous people in the world are probably also the most envious is one of the many paradoxes of the Spanish makeup" (Diaz-Playa, 1967, p. 167).

It is due to an excess of individualism and a deficiency in social values that envy is so widespread in Spain. Gracián calls it malignidad hispana.... Enviousness, together with the isolation in which Spain tends to live, will not allow her to see in the unity of other nations the qualities necessary for success" (Menéndez Pidal, 1946/1966, pp. 51, 66).

Several excellent essays have been written on the Spanish envy. It is, obviously, one of our "national vices." (López Ibor, 1969, p. 26).

Arabs are also plagued with envy, from their equally strong sense of *honor/honra*

Aggression is also manifested through the preponderance of hasad (envy) and jealousy among the Arabs" (Hamady, 12960, p. 43).

Both the Badawin and his women are envious to a degree, and cupidity is the breath of life to them. Both are as full of *hasad* and *tamá* (envy and cupidity) as anyone in this world could be, and they never tire of saying that others around them suffer from these vices but never themselves. *Hasad* takes the form of backbiting at every opportunity, and disparaging the efforts and good name of anyone who happens to be better off" (Dickson, 1951, p. 56).

A non Madariagan explanation

Menéndez Pidal writes that envy "is due to an excess of individualism and a deficiency in social values." However, while individualism has grown significantly in recent centuries in all modern countries, this has not caused a parallel increase in envy. On the contrary, as envy prospers in a collective world in which everybody pays attention to what others say and do, envy diminishes in an individualistic world where people are less controlling and judgemental.

My explanation of high levels of envy is different from Menendez Pidal's and corresponds with that given by the *Dizionario*

Enciclopedico Italiano and the *New Catholic Encyclopaedia*[8] —in which envy is linked to pride.

Envy as the direct consequence of pride in one's *linaje y honra*, and a corresponding lack of emphasis on personal development and success through initiative, creativity, risk, hard work, trial and error. Therefore, if others are more and have more, it means one of two things:

1. They were better at birth (and this is an insult for those less fortunate); or
2. They cheated, and have what they do not deserve. Probably their lineage is fake, it was obtained by cheating, or they are not the legitimate branch.

In either case, there is no reason why others should be more, or have more; and precisely this "no reason" is the source of envy. In other words, if others have more, it is an insult to one's honor, it is an attack on one's honra which must be cleansed.

Part of the explanation is related to a disdain for work: In a world in which *linaje y honra* are paramount, one who makes his fortune through his industry is an ugly *nouveau riche*, a despicable *parvenu*. The only fine-smelling fortune is the inherited one. Indeed, those who have inherited well must have done so because of their intrinsic value.

8. In praise of Madariaga

Anticipating my final conclusion, let me pay homage to Madariaga who has written a great book on national characters. I may have been harsh on him, but without his book, our discourse on characters would have been limited and less clear. We need a strong thesis to develop an equally strong anti-thesis and synthesis.

---

[8]   "Envy is the feeling of rancorous pain which is felt for somebody else's goods, often joined with the wish that these may convert themselves in misfortune; also the general disposition to feel such a feeling, *due, quite often, to a sense of pride* by which one does not tolerate that others should have talents equal or better, or have more success in their activities or more luck" (*Dizionario Enciclopedico Italiano*, 1957, 6, p. 294, my italics). "The envious person is saddened because he feels lessened and humiliated when another is more favored than himself" (*New Catholic Encyclopaedia*, 1967, v, p. 451).

6

Barzini's *Mutable Germans* Explained

1. Mutable?

In *The Europeans* of 1983, Luigi Barzini described the character of the Germans in a chapter "The Mutable Germans". The other chapters are: "The Imperturbable British," "The Quarrelsome French," "The Flexible Italians," "The Careful Dutch, and "The Baffling Americans."

Barzini calls Germany a "trompe l'oeil Protean country.... Every time I was there on a journalistic mission, I saw a startling new country, only vaguely resembling what I had seen before or what I had read about....I was aware there must have been a constant basic Germany, whose virtues and vices practically went unchanged from one metamorphosis to the next, from one regime to its successor, from one political, philosophic, or aesthetic fashion to another. But it was difficult,... It is still difficult for foreigners, and for the Germans themselves. What is the shape of Proteus when caught unaware at rest?" (pp. 69-71).

What is the shape of the German Proteus when caught unaware? My answer is that his basic shape is (or was through the 1960s) that of a *ritter* (knight/soldier). Behind the many metamorphoses, I see an all pervading *ritter*-character "whose virtues and vices practically went unchanged from one metamorphosis to the next, from one regime to its successor," which manifests itself differently in function of different cultural, economic and political conditions. During bourgeois non-*ritter* times, his *ritter*-character goes into hiding, only to quickly reemerge during nationalistic, pro-*ritter* times.

This *ritter* character not only differentiates the Germans, past and present, from other peoples such as the British, French, Italians, Dutch, Americans, but gives the Germans a degree of continuity, of *immutability*, which other peoples don't have. It is a paradox, but only an apparent one, that the people who seem so mutable are, in reality, the most constant behind a series of superficial changes.

It is true that the Germans often give the impression of changing: from being unwarlike and *gemütlich* as noted by Madame de Staël in her *De l'Allemagne* of 1810: "Nothing is odder than the German soldiers,... They fear fatigue or bad weather, as if they were all shopkeepers or literati" (quoted by Barzini, 1983, p. 72) to the daring and efficient soldiers of Blücher at Ligny-Waterloo or the disciplined, relentless unstoppable spiked helmets of the 1870 war against France.

Barzini quoted another, earlier, peaceful, unwarlike description of the Germans, this time by Machiavelli in his *Ritratto delle Cose della Magna* [Portrait on the State of Germany] of 1512: "*E così si godono questa rozza vita e libertà; e per questa causa non vogliono ire alla guerra.*" (Thus they enjoy their rough life and their liberty, and do not want to go to war) (1983, p. 72). Yet, a mere fifteen years later, the fierce *Landsknechte* from Germany sacked Rome in 1527: "The atrocities and profanations they committed far exceeded those inflicted in the past by Goths or Vandals, Saracens or Normans" (Cheetham, 1982, p. 201).

A careful reading of Machiavelli might have told Barzini not to stress the "do not want to go to war." Two paragraphs earlier, he would have read that: "*In soldati non spendono, perché tengono li uomini loro armati ed esercitati; e li giorni delle feste tali uomini, in cambio delli giochi, chi si esercita allo scoppietto, chi colla pica, e chi con una arme e chi con una altra*" (1966, p. 821) (They do not spend money for soldiers, because they keep their men armed and trained; and on festive days those men, instead of playing games, exercise, some with rifles, some with pikes, some with one weapon and some with another). Those Germans may not have wanted to go to war, but they were very well prepared for it. In other words, even in peaceful times, their life was embedded in a *ritter* ethnopsychology.Given a good reason to wage war, they did it with gusto and efficiency. Even if they did not want war, when called to duty they knew how to perform.

Thomas Mann also discovered this kind of changeability when, in his novel *Lotte in Weimar*, he commented on the rapid evolution of the German personality during the Napoleonic timesthrough the voice of Adele Schopenhauer: "One must admit that he [Napoleon] changed the Germans very much. He turned their milk—that is to say, their homely, pious ways of give and take—into boiling dragon's blood; and he even made a grim patriot and soldier of freedom out of the versatile humanist von Humboldt. Shall we account it a merit or a crime in Caesar, that he changed our minds and brought us to ourselves? I will not judge" (1939, p. 184). The phrase "brought us to ourselves," is significant! Even the versatile humanist changed rapidly, as did Thomas Mann with his highly patriotic *Reflections of a Nonpolitical Man* of 1918.

2. The main characteristics of the *ritter* character

The main characteristics of the *ritter* (knight/warrior) character are: fidelity, courage, hard work, discipline in following orders or in setting the example, energy and endurance, perfectionism and pedantry, heroism, pride, arrogance, hate of compromise, will to power, superhumanism, greediness, anger and rage, ferocity and cruelty, a certain love for pomp and uniforms, love for the romantic, tendency to theorize, obsession with the ideal. Obviously, for a given person, each of them will be present in different proportions, many not at all, yet their sum-integration should differentiate a large number of Germans from say a large number of Britons, French, Italians, Dutch, and Americans. Many of these are positive traits, virtues which most people should strive for. Sadly however, many of these traits can quickly transform into negative traits when in the service of nefarious leaders or a tyrannical society. On the other hand, whenever these virtues are put to work, in a just free society, they have produced wonders. Germans abroad have often done admirably. Away from home it was easier for them to chose which ideal to follow, which program to serve or lead.

3. Fidelity

Fidelity is the main virtue of the *ritter* (knight)world, highly praised, constantly preached and demanded unconditionally by every lord. Only in this way could the lord avoid insubordination, neglect of duties, betrayals or coups d'état. As long as each lord was in constant warfare with his neighbors or with his overlord (as was the case in Germany and Japan), he had to maintain a ready army, staffed with faithful and trained warriors, ready to intervene at any moment, capable of using their initiative within a clearly understood overall scheme. "The more able a knight was as a warrior, the more dangerous he might be if he lacked loyalty. Thus prowess and loyalty were the great feudal virtues." (Painter, 1961, p. 101).

Fidelity was also of paramount importance in Japan

The prime virtue in the Japanese feudal system, as in that of Europe, was loyalty, because the whole system depended on bonds of personal loyalty.... The lord-vassal relationship was seen as one of unlimited and absolute loyalty on the part of the vassal, not merely one of legal contract between the two.... Loyalty to the ruler was important in the Chinese Confucian system, but it was usually overshadowed by loyalty to the family.... In Japan, loyalty to the lord was more central to the whole system and, despite the importance of the family, took precedence over loyalty to it. (Reischauer, 1977, p. 57)

A famous example of fidelity was given by 47 *ronin* (masterless samurai) in 1703 in Edo (Tokyo). They ambushed the nobleman who had caused their master's suicide, cut his head and carried it to the Buddhist temple where their lord was buried, and offered it before his grave. Surrendering thereafter to the Shogun, they were ordered to commit suicide which they did, showing fidelity first to their Lord, then to the Shogun they had offended by taking justice into their hands. The affair has been immortalized in more than one hundred plays.[9]

An interesting feature is that at no moment in the initial renditions of the story was there any mention of Lord Asano deserving the loyalty of his retainers by the sterling administration of his people. Some even have asserted that Lord Asano was avaricious and cruel, and that his troubles arose from his refusal to compensate Lord Kira generously for his expertise. This was told to stress how the loyalty of his samurai, later declassed ronin, was absolute. "The whole point of the play [Chushingura] is the unconditional nature of loyalty" (Keene, 1971, p. 17).[10]

4. The misuse of fidelity

However, as soon as we praise the pluses of fidelity, we also see its dark side: its abuse for less illustrious purposes. In the most eminent of the German sagas, the Nibelungenlied—a Middle High German epic poem written by an unknown Austrian poet from the Danube region—we encounter a striking example of the misuse of fidelity,

---

[9] The most famous play is *Chûshingura* by Takeda Izumo of 1748. (Chûshingura means "very obedient" or more specifically "a group of very obedient people.") To this day, the Japanese honor to the fidelity and heroism of the 47 ronin by visiting their graves in the garden of the Sengakuji temple in Tokyo.

[10] Another point is the *partial-unity of power:* The story had its beginnings in "an established custom under the Tokugawa rule (1603-1868) for the Shogun to present annually to the Imperial Court in Kyoto a large sum of money and other gifts as a token of the New Year's greetings, and for the Emperor to despatch in return his envoys to the Yedo Castle to inquire after the Shogun's health. On such occasions the Shogun's government appointed customarily from among the daimyos or feudal lords, three hundred in number, two officers to attend to the Imperial envoys" (Sakae, 1956, p. 9). One of these two daimyos was Lord Asano who ran into trouble with Lord Kira, the expert in court ceremonial, and wounded him. In consequence, Asano was condemned to commit suicide, his property was confiscated, the family name was erased, and his samurai became ronin.
We read of large sums and other gifts sent by the Shogun to the Emperor who then sends his envoys to inquire about the Shogun's health. And we read of an important role played yearly, on rotation, by two out of the 300 feudal lords in honoring the envoys of the Emperor. While this was not full *division of power*, as proven by the suicides of Lord Asano and his ronin, it was neither full *unity of power*: it was a feudal *partial unity of power*, not much different from the German system; both are based on the same high number of semi-independent principalities.

when Queen Kriemhilde—in her revenge for the killing of her former husband, Siegfried—demanded that Margrave Rüdiger kill his Burgundian friends, the three kings Gunther, Gernot and Giselher. "Now came Kriemhilde, and appealed to Rüdiger: 'You often pledged honor and life for us, and when you asked my hand for king Etzel, you swore to always serve me faithfully. I now remind you of this oath, for never have I needed your fidelity more than now....Rüdiger bewailed 'Woe is me! Why must this come upon me! I hosted the Burgundian kings in my house, I gave my daughter in marriage to Giselher. I am bound to them by fidelity. How could I send them to their death? Yet, to you also I swore fidelity. Whatever I do, whatever I omit, I will always infringe on my duty and my honor." Rüdiger fought in his heart a difficult battle. But there was no escape, and he said to King Etzel: "'The fidelity which I swore to you with my feudal oath is unbreakable." And thus the Duke put on his armor and went with his knights to the hall, resolute to keep his feudal fidelity to King Etzel, but also resolute to die in the battle against the Burgundians" (*Die Nibelungen*, 1978, p. 167-8; *Das Nibelungenlied*, verses 2147-68). The terrible unjust and senseless carnage continued, until all the Burgundians lay dead.

Fifty years later, *Der getreue Wolfdietrich* (The faithful Wolfdietrich), another famous saga, was written. Again, on page two, we encounter the tragic misuse of fidelity: "Berchtung von Meran was secretly called by King Hugdietrich who so spoke to him: 'You must kill my young son, so secretly that nobody will ever know it.' The faithful knight answered: 'Oh, no!God spare me this! I will never be guilty of his death!' Said the King: 'Remember that you are my most faithful servant! But if you refuse my request, our joint fidelity must come to an end. In Lilienporte you have a beautiful wife, and sixteen handsome sons. I will have them all hanged on the battlements, but first of all you.' The faithful knight thought: 'He is in a bad mood. If I do not do as he wants, he will do as he threatened.' Thus he spoke to the king: 'If you will not spare me, I must kill the child" (*Deutsche Heldensagen*, 1937, pp. 186-187).[11]

---

[11]   Ultimately the King's son was not killed. As in the fairy tale Snow White, when Berchtung was alone in the wood, he took pity on the boy and took him with great secrecy to live with a lonely, elderly couple. Berchtung called the boy Wolfdietrich because of his courage with the wolves.

Literature was not far from real life. For instance, Peter Amelung in his *Portrait of the Germans in the Italian literature of the Renaissance* reported that for the Italians of the Middle Ages, "The discipline and fidelity of the Germans were nothing to be proud of, because both made them into blind tools of their lords" (1964, p. 33).

More recently, fidelity became the most prized virtue of the Third Reich: every member of the Nazi Party, every soldier, and finally every German had to swear fidelity to Hitler. Therefore, Heinrich Himmler set fidelity at the foundation of the SS. "Heinrich went even further and made the vague notion of *Treue* [fidelity] synonymous with the upholding of all his beliefs on sexual behavior and political activity, regardless of the social consequences or the opinions of others. Gradually Treue came to be focused on the absolute necessity of carrying out the wishes of the party and its *Führer*, Adolf Hitler. The slogan of the SS, Meine *Ehre heisst Treue* [My honor is fidelity], marked the institutionalization of this concept inside the Nazi system. But if the heart of one's value system is party *Treue*, then what actions are to be regarded as proof of one's virtue? Certainly not the actions performed in obedience to orders of the kind that most men are willing to obey. Only by the willing execution of orders and the assumption of responsibilities that others find immoral or distasteful can one truly demonstrate the highest commitment to *Treue*" (B. F. Smith, 1971, p. 171).

Joachim Fest (1974) was shocked by how the Nazis appropriated the best (ritter) virtues of "loyalty, honesty, obedience, hardness, decency, poverty, and bravery. But all these virtues were detached from any comprehensive frame of reference and directed entirely toward the purposes of the regime" (p. 377). This became terribly evident, in the Leni Riefenstahl film *Triumph of the Will*, when Rudolf Hess put the masses on fire with his: "The Party is Hitler, and Hitler is Germany."

Rudolf Hess could have equally said, that "The Army is Hitler," because, in that same year, Hitler bound the Army to his person in a way that would have won the praise of all German emperors from Charlemagne to Wilhelm II. To leave no loopholes Hitler exacted from all officers and men of the armed forces an oath of allegiance— not to Germany, not to the constitution, which he had violated by not calling for the election of Hindenburg's successor[12], but to himself. It read:

> I swear by God this sacred oath, that I will render uncon-ditional obedience to Adolf Hitler, the Fuehrer of the German Reich and people, Supreme Commander of the Armed Forc-es, and will be ready as a brave soldier to risk my life at any time for this oath.'

> From August 1934 on, the generals, who up to that time could have overthrown the NaziRegimewith ease had they so desired, thus tied themselves to the person of Adolf Hitler, recognizing him as the highest legitimate authority in the land and binding themselves to him by an oath of fealty which they felt honor-bound to obey in all circumstances no matter how degrading to them and the Fatherland. It was an oath which was to trouble the conscience of quite a few high officers when their acknowledged leader set off on a path which they opposed. It was also a pledge which enabled an even greater number of officers to excuse themselves from any personal responsibility for the unspeakable crimes which they carried out on the orders of a Supreme Commander whose true na-ture they had seen for themselves in the butchery of June 30 [1934]. (Shirer, 1960, pp. 226-7)

One of the most famous generals who found himself bound by the oath of fidelity was Field-Marshall Erwin Rommel, who, already during World War I, had earned the most prestigious German military award, *Pour le Mérite*.

> Like the marriage vow he had sworn to Lucie in Dan-zig in 1917, the oath of allegiance he and every officer had sworn to the Führer in 1934 was inhibiting enough to prevent a man of Rommel's convictions from actually "cheating" [i.e. revolting against Hitler]. Besides, he and the active field-mar-shals had personally signed a second testimony of allegiance

---

[12] In America the military oath is: "I, ..., do solemnly swear that I will support and defend the Constitution of the United States against all enemies, foreign and domestic. That I will bear true faith and allegiance to the same. .... So help me God."

to Hitler in March 1944. Non-Germans may find it difficult
to accept that upstanding generals could become tyrannized
by their own oath of allegiance. But they were—their entire
careers had been dominated by it and by the ethos that superior orders have to be obeyed. Victories had flowed from it,
defeats had been impeded. Rommel demanded instant obedience from his juniors, and he liked to believe he was an
obedient man himself. Had he not written in July 1941 to his
commander-in-chief, Brauchitsch: 'Above all I must demand
from my officers that they set an example and obey.' Had he
not sternly advised his own son, Manfred, in December 1943:
'Obey without question!'" (Irving, 1977, pp. 408-9)

It would be wrong to accept, without qualification, the comments by David Irving. The dichotomy is not between non-Germans
who find it difficult to accept that upstanding generals could become
tyrannized by their own oath of allegiance, and Germans who could
understand it. The dichotomy is not between generals and civilians.
The dichotomy is between *ritter* people and *ritter* regimes (which
include many Japanese, and most Fascist regimes) on one side, and
non-ritter people and non-*ritter* regimes (e.g. *visitors* and *insulars*,
and democracies) on the other. The German generals may have been
more *ritter* than the civilians, but much of their personality had been
shaped not by the Army but by their national culture from infancy
onward. When Rommel sternly advised his son Manfred to "Obey
without question!" he spoke first as father, and then as field-marshall.

5. Courage and bravery

Once fidelity is assured, the lord demands and praises courage, because only courage will lead his vassals to great deeds. Only
their courage and bravery will bring him victory over his enemies.
Correspondingly he will promote the heroic script which teaches that
"Only in the face of the most fearful adversities will the hero show his
mettle. [And that] Honor and fidelity, and fearless bravery are incon-
testable values" (Fricke, 1951, p. 11). At the popular level, fairy tales
sang the praise of courage, and listed the great honors and the many
gifts that would be its reward: the king's beautiful daughter and the
royal crown. Courage is the main theme of Grimms' The boy *who left
home to find out about shivers:* The King had promised his daughter,

the most beautiful maiden under the sun, in marriage to the man who could spend three nights in the bewitched castle. On top, the successful man would become king. Similarly, in *The Brave Little Tailor*, courage won the King's beautiful daughter and half the kingdom.

Similar praise for courage is found in the old sagas: Siegfried is defined as "the fearless man," and young Wolfdietrich saved his life because he "did not know fear" when surrounded by wolves. Siegfried's courage is the central theme of Act I of Wagner's opera by the same name, when the Wanderer/Wotan tells Mime that only the "One who has never learnt to fear" will make anew the sword Notung, and with it destroy the dragon Fafner. Mime then tries to teach fear to Siegfried but to no avail.

However, lords soon learned how to reward courage and bravery with cheaper carrots: a title, a medal, a friendly word, or only a nod. Thomas Mann had a good understanding of this last method when his Marquis de Venosta (alias Felix Krull) related how he generously dealt with the train conductor: "I gave him a gracious smile and a nod *de haut en bas* that assuredly confirmed him in his conservative principles to the point where he would gladly have fought and bled for them" (1958, p. 232).

As with fidelity, the dark side of courage and bravery is not fear or pusillanimity but its abuse in the hands of a heartless lord who sets inhuman tasks, as did the king in Schiller's poem "The diver":

The king then seizes the goblet in haste,
In the gulf he hurls it with might;
"When the goblet once more in my hands thou hast placed,
Thou shalt rank at my court as the noblest knight,
And her[13] as bride thou shalt clasp e'en to-day,
Who for thee with tender compassion doth pray."
....
For life or for death, lo! he plunges him in!
....
And the waters are pouring in fast around;

---

[13]   The king's daughter.

Though upwards and downwards they rush and they rave,
The youth is brought back by no kindly wave. (1797/1900,
p. 172)

6. Hard work and thoroughness

For centuries the Germans have been famous for their diligence and
thoroughness, qualities important for any achievement, be it in industry
and commerce, technology and science, the arts, ... war and persecution.

Already in the Renaissance, as reported by John Hale, Giovanni
Paolo Lomazzo portrayed the Germans as careful workers and faithful
soldiers, and Fynes Morryson praised the Germans for "their skill as
artificers, but added 'I think that to be attributed not to their sharpness
of whit, but to their industry'" (1994, p. 61).

But why should these virtues be ritter? Because for centuries,
and even today, good instructions and examples, close supervision,
and a robust system of reward and punishment produce wonders. For
centuries, people progressed under the motto of *Initium perfectionis
(aut sapientiae) timor domini* (The fear of the Lord is the beginning
of wisdom, *Psalms 111:10)*, which the Germans translated freely into
"Das Auge des Herrn macht die Kühe fett" (The eye of the master
fattens the cow).

Life in a castle—ruled by an active lord who set the example,
rewarded his best knights, neglected or punished the less capable or
less enterprising—fostered schooling and training, hard work and
thoroughness, courage and fidelity. German margraves and Japanese
daimyos knew this perfectly well: any slackness could meandefeat
and death. Any lack of fidelity, courage or diligence, were therefore
high treason with dire consequences for everybody.

7. Ritter Kant

Discusssion of the *ritter character* of the Germans acquires a
deeper meaning when it is seen in the works of their greatest philosopher, Kant (with explanatory *ritter comments*, from another eminent
German philosopher, Schopenhauer)

On the need of a Master, in Kant's own words:

> Man is an animal which, if it lives among others of its kind, requires a master. For he certainly abuses his freedom with respect to other men, and although as a reasonable being he wishes to have a law which limits the freedom of all, his selfish animal impulses tempt him where possible, to exempt himself from them. *He thus requires a master, who will break his will and force him to obey a will that is universally valid,* under which each can be free. But whence does he get this master? Only from the human race. But the master is himself an animal, and needs a master. Let him begin as he will, it is not to be seen how he can procure a magistracy which maintain public justice and which is itself just, whether it be a single person or a group of several elected persons. *For each of them will always abuse his freedom if he has none above him to exercise force in accord with the law.* The highest master should be just in himself, and yet a man. This task is therefore the hardest of all; *indeed, its complete solution is impossible, from such crooked wood as man is made of, nothing perfectly straight can be built.* (1784/1963, p. 17-18; my italics)

Thus, according to Kant, each of us requires a master in charge of breaking our will and forcing us to obey a will that is universally valid. That master is needed because we all are made of *crooked wood*[14] from which nothing perfectly straight can be built.

In turn "Schopenhauer [who] thought that he alone had understood Kant correctly, and dismissed Kant's other successors, especially Hegel, as charlatans"[15], said clearly that the master was nobody else but the king, who

> became the firm unshakable pillar on which alone the entire legal order and thus the rights of all repose and continue to exist. But he can perform this role only by virtue of the

---

[14]   The source of the title of Isaiah Berlin's *The crooked timber of humanity: Chapters in the History of Ideas* of 1991.

[15]   Hollingdale, 1970, p. 20.

inborn prerogative which *bestows upon him and only him an authority above every other which cannot be doubted or contested and which, indeed, everyone obeys as if by instinc*t. Thus he is rightly called "by the grace of God", and is at all times the most useful person in the state, whose services cannot be rewarded too highly by any civil list, no matter how costly. (1851/1970, p. 151; my italics)

The king (or other great leader) is that master charged with breaking our will and forcing us to *obey a [ritter] will that is universally valid*, i.e. his will.

10. And today?

The Germans of today seem to have left their old *ritter* character-behind, and become the standard-bearer of a united, democratic and socially progressive Europe. They are against wars and militarism, and dislike uniforms of any kind. Yet, could this be another of their protean transformations? Should we fear that *Sleeping Beauty* will be awakened once more by the kiss of a daring prince?

7

Therivel's *Visitor* vs. *Insular* Cultures Explained

1. Introduction

The type of power, whether united or divided, exercised over a society for a long period of time has a profound influence on individual personality development, on the evolution of culture and mentalities, and on creativity at the personal and societal levels.

The difference in psychological and social characteristics, and resulting types of civilization deriving from either a single source of power or a divided one, is so fundamental as to demand the creation of two new psychological terms. The proposed terms for theoretical and practical applications, are *insular* and *visitor*. The first refers to the personality type or form of civilization that evolved under the oppression of one single, unified source of power. The second refers to the result of the impact of a multiplicity of sources of conflicting powers.

The psychological characteristics of the *insular* and *visitor* personalities are presented in Table 1, and can be used to broadly divide people or civilizations. For instance, the terms *insular* and *visitor* can be used for an additional understanding of the development of the personal and social philosophy of most later-period Chinese and many Latin-Americans as *insulars,* and of most Western Europeans and North Americans as *visitors*.

Summary of *Visitor* Versus *Insular* Personality Characteristics, Division of Power (DP) or Unity of Power (UP)

Visitor (shaped by DP)	Insular (shaped by UP)
Is / Has / Does / Believes In / Favors	
Critical thinker, especially of leaders and stale traditions	Uncritical thinker
Independent, self-directed, self-sufficient, confident	Dependent, conformist, knowing one's place, intolerant of nonconformity
Going places and taking risks	Staying put and playing it safe
Frankness and speaking one's mind	Silence and dissimulation
Controlling one's life	Controlled or controlling others
Assertive	Acquiescent
Optimist	Pessimist
Dialogue, negotiations, and checks and balances	Submission or imposition, inquisition and discipline of others
Separation, justice perspective, detailed laws, recourse to legal fights	Connection, caring perspective, compromise, patriarchal or imperial fiat
Less centered on family and clan	More centered on family and clan
Democracy and federalism	Aristocracy and central government
Initiator or volunteer for the good	Leaves initiative to group or state, or is conscript and draftee

Revolutionary and creative (especially in philosophy, religion, politics, science)	Conservative and less creative (especially in philosophy, religion, politics, science.)

The study of the causes at the root of these two fundamental types can help to explain why Western civilization (and its prolonged high level of creativity, especially in the scientific and humanitarian areas) is so different from any other in the history of the world. This chapter, therefore, presents at the same time the results of a study on the development of individual and group personalities, types of power, places and times of creativity, and comments on the origin and evolution of the Western civilization.

2. In Short

The *insular personality* is the result of a life (particularly a youth) spent in a society ruled by one domineering power (emperor, king, party secretary), where this power is not restricted by any major division—when there is no possibility of maneuver, for the individual or the group, by switching allegiance to another power. *Insular* people know that they have no recourse or escape, and that they must stay in the good graces of the power holder or that their only alternative is to fight and seize power, something not available to many. Under these conditions, *insulars* must learn to show a good face and never exhibit unhappiness, hatred or a desire to revolt, because the power holder will crush them and nobody will come to their rescue. Patience and dissimulation, silence and accommodation must be their virtues, which are strongly engraved in their mental scripts.

Visitors, instead, know that they can always resort to Power Holder A, who will welcome new supporters in the fight against Power Holder B. In modern times this means having recourse to the legislative power if things go wrong with the executive, or appeal for help from the judiciary, the press or media, one of the political parties, from unions, or from churches. Visitors, operating in a *division of power* (DP) environment, know that they can never be badly harmed, never be crushed, because somebody will come to their aid. Consequently, *visitors* have faith in themselves as persons in control of important aspects of their lives, which in turn gives them faith in their autonomy. They may therefore take risks, even against the power closest to them.

3. *Insular*

Without recourse against the power holder, *insular* persons must protect themselves through ties at their own level and at the hierarchical levels below them. Therefore, *insulars* place great emphasis on family ties. Only the closest relatives (parents, spouse, children) will help them in case of trouble; the family must be united; the family must be the secure haven where the hated mask of smiling obedience can be removed. The children must know that they can count on their parents, regardless of what happens to them. The father—exposed to the boss—must count on total fidelity and obedience from wife and children. This is imperative for survival. If at all possible, the parents will seek to secure alliances within the extended family or the clan. In a country under *unity of power* (UP) no one can ever be assured of one's position, because every power holder will have a tyrant above him in a continuum which leads to the ultimate power holder, for instance, the emperor, who in turn can never feel safe because too many vie for his power. To protect himself, every power holder will preach the virtues of fidelity, of "knowing one's place," of complete obedience and love. The emperor or pope or clan leader will present himself as "father," and the father will demand to be the emperor of his family.

Once this is taken into account, the existence of contrasting reports of basic insular behavior (e.g., "impassivity/inscrutability" versus "emotivity/friendship") can be understood. The explanation lies in "with whom and where," as shown in the following comments on the tripartite division of all social relations among Chinese by professor Yang Kuo-shu, as reported by Kleinman and Kleinman (1991):

> The nearest compartment is occupied by family and close friends. Here, trust is unconditional, and certain private feelings can be revealed. The second compartment contains distant family and friends. Here trust is conditional, and feelings will only occasionally be expressed, and always with great caution. The most distant compartment contains relations with strangers. Here there is an absolute lack of trust, and inner experience is not to be expressed lest it is used against one's family and social network. . . . Demonstrating strong feelings, including the menaced and aggrieved affects of suffering, is dangerous, because it gives others power over

relationships and restricts one's flexibility to respond effectively. Ultimately, uncontrolled emotional displays threaten one's position in a world of power. (p. 288)

These are the personal *Weltanschauungen* and life strategies of most Chinese of the recent past and the present, in a country where formerly the emperor and now the Communist Party, held undisputed power; in a country famous for its strong family ties and its almost worshipful respect and devotion to parents and ancestors.

Mexico's leading poet, Nobel laureate, essayist, and cultural critic, Octavio Paz (1950/1985), noticed common characteristics between Mexicans and Chinese:

> Our hermeticism is baffling or even offensive to strangers, and it has created the legend of the Mexican as an inscrutable being. Our suspicions keep us at a distance. . . . The impression we create is much like that created by Orientals. They too—the Chinese, the Hindus, the Arabs—are hermetic and indecipherable. (p. 65)

For Paz, Mexicans shut themselves away and wear a mask because they instinctively regard the world as dangerous: "It is revealing that our intimacy never flowers in a natural way, only when incited by fiestas, alcohol, or death. Slaves, servants, and submerged races always wear a mask, whether smiling or sullen" (p.70). After having stressed that this reaction is justifiable in view of the history of the Mexicans, Paz made a remark about them that is nearly identical to that reported by Kleinman and Kleinman about the Chinese: "Only when they are alone, during the great moments of life, do they dare to show themselves as they are. All their relationships are poisoned by fear and suspicion: fear of the master and suspicion of their equals. Each keeps watch over the other because every companion could also be a traitor" (p.70).

For Arabic city-dwellers, the family is the state, a be-all-and-end-all in itself, where every child grows up feeling that his prime responsibility is not toward society but toward his family or, in the words of Vatikiotis (1987):

family; it is the principal intermediary between the individual and his social-cultural milieu. Such values as authoritarianism, respect for seniority, male dominance, overdependence on social milieu and status, helplessness *vis-à-vis* state power and lack of personal initiative are still widely, overwhelmingly prevalent (p.70).

Barzini (1965) made similar comments on the *insulars* of southern Italy:

> The Italian family is a stronghold in a hostile land: within its walls and among its members, the individual finds consolation, help, advice, provisions, loans, weapons, allies and accomplices to aid him in his pursuit. No Italian who has a family is ever alone. He finds in it a refuge in which to lick his wounds after a defeat, or an arsenal and a staff for his victorious drives. . . . This is, of course, nothing new, surprising, or unique. In many countries and among many people, past and present, where legal authority is weak and the law is resented, the safety and welfare of the individual are mainly assured by the family. The Chinese, for instance, in their imperial days held the cult of the family more praiseworthy than the love of country and the love of good. . . . The family extracts everybody's first loyalty. It must be defended, enriched, made powerful, respected, and feared by the use of whatever means are necessary, legitimate means, if at all possible, or illegitimate. (pp. 198-201)

4. *Visitor*

North-Americans are visitors par excellence living in the country which has had the greatest division of power in the world for the last two centuries. In the last quarter of the eighteenth century, no nation in the world was governed by officially defined separated and divided powers providing checks and balances on the exercise of authority by those who governed. The Declaration of Independence of 1776 was a first step toward this division, followed by the Constitution of 1787 and the Bill of Rights of 1791. Each had antecedents back to the English Bill of Rights, the Magna Carta, and the Investiture Controversy of 1075-1122. With this background of a strong division of power in the United States we can understand why, in the words of Diaz-Guer-rero and Diaz-Loving (1990):

> Being dominant and dictatorial. . . . is perceived as an undesirable instrumental characteristic for U.S. subjects—bad for both sexes, but worse for females—[and] perceived in Mexico as positive instrumental traits, desirable in both sexes but better in males. The importance given in Mexico to showing respect and affectionate obedience toward parents and older people in general seems not only to make it acceptable to be authoritarian, but actually encourages it. Other traits, such as being aggressive, which in the United States is desirable for males and not for females, are seen as generally negative in both sexes in Mexico, although more undesirable in females. . . . even assertiveness is not a positive characteristic in Mexico. . . . Mexicans tend to be self-modifying rather than other-modifying. Aggression, and even assertiveness, are other-modifying behaviors. Further evidence is provided by the fact that the item "servile," which is a negative expressive trait in the United States, is a positive expressive characteristic in Mexico. (pp. 519-20)

Here we have, in a nutshell, the description of the North American *visitor* and the Mexican *insular*.

5. Transmission by Cultural Continuity

Ethnopsychologies are stable and evolve only slowly under the impact of major changes in the power structure from UP to DP or vice versa. Once firmly established by a given power structure, the *visitor* or *insular* personality will be transmitted to subsequent generations by cultural continuity or inertia. This is illustrated in two studies (Harwood and Miller 1991; Harwood and Lucca Irizarry 1992) of what contemporary American and Puerto Rican mothers considered acceptable conduct in their children. American mothers placed value on child characteristics such as being active, independent, curious, and capable of self-enhancement—traits that will permit the child to confront new situations in an autonomous way. Puerto Rican mothers, instead, valued characteristics such as being quiet, respectful, and obedient—traits that will permit the child to behave in an adequate and dignified way in a public context.

These results are in line with observations by Rogelio Diaz-Guer-rero, research professor at the Faculty of Psychology of the Universidad Nacional Autónoma de México, in his *Psychology of the Mexican: Culture and Personality*: "Ultimately, the historical traditional pattern of the United States will produce individuals who are active. . . . independent, individualistic, autonomous, oriented toward achievement, competitive, somewhat impulsive and aggressive, and rather tense and nervous. The Mexican historical-sociocultural pattern, on the other hand, will produce individuals who are obedient, affiliative, interdependent, orderly, cooperative, not oriented toward achievement, and not self-initiated. . . . [And on raising children,] Slowly in the first two years and then under intensive pressure, the infant must become well brought up, *bien educado*. They must become model children who will perforce fit into the system of absolute obedience to the parents. This necessary obedience, humility, and respect to the elders and for authority are imposed in a great many ways. Drilling in courtesy and in manners is a prevalent one" (1967/1975, p. xvii, 9-10).

6. *Insular* Less Creative

The *insular* personality is less creative at each of the three systems of Csikszentmihalyi's "triangular locus of creativity"(1988): *person, domain* (symbol system), *field* (social organization of domain). In terms of the *person, insulars* have less insight/inspiration that comes from "seeing the world in a new and different light" (Weiten, 1989, p. 292), because their strong scripts tell them how to assimilate new information, in line with the old, instead of how to understand it as something truly new. In consequence, insulars are pleased with the old, fundamental elements of their world; if there are problems, they derive from a lack of faith in and fidelity to the tradition. This repression of the new avoids the need for unpalatable accommodations, but it also eliminates creativity.

In an *insular* world, the *field* blesses only those works which fit the approved truth/ tradition/ scripts. In consequence, anything new is refused and excommunicated, with no hiding place and little opportunity to move to an independent field free to appreciate and protect it. Ultimately, the *insular* person has no incentive to put the famous 99 percent of perspiration behind his or her unorthodox 1 percent of inspiration. Similar considerations apply to the insular domain, which consists of rigid themes and exacting performance rules.

An example of this is the *insular* personality of the ancient Egyptians of the later dynasties, who had lived for centuries under the pharaoh's supreme unity of civilian, economic, and religious power as manifested in the constancy of their *domain*: "In techniques, art, and writing, the methods developed in the earliest times remained, in general terms, satisfactory for the needs of the Egyptian people and over the centuries required only the modifications resulting from natural development within a fairly closed culture. This self-sufficiency. . . . amounted almost to a sort of cultural stagnation" (T. James, 1978, p. 460).

In essence, *insular* people are less creative because they are subject to a single truth linked intrinsically to one single power.

7. The Origins of the Division of Power in the West

The modern visitor personality was born at the end of the eleventh century, when two fundamental powers, papacy and empire, preaching different ontological/epistemological truths, began to oppose each other in a major *war of the scripts*. The resulting creative revolution led to new evolving truths, different from those fabricated by each of the two powers, more humane, and closer to scientific truth, because they arose in a broader dialectic world, less subservient to either of the great powers.

This *war of the scripts* was possible because, for the first time in history, a series of unarmed religious leaders (popes) successfully opposed the lay rulers (emperors and kings).

Western civilization is different from every other civilization, not only because of its complex Judaic, Greek, Roman, Germanic roots, but also because it was formed from the synergy of a monotheistic religion, not founded by a military commander, and the special geographic/historical/cultural/political role played by Rome as the seat of the popes. The notion of a single God legitimizes the idea of a single underlying universal truth and unitary paradigms and excludes, a priori, a "religious" division of power among leaders of the cult of different gods. For centuries, the popes were the leaders of the only religion of the West, which gave them enormous power. Furthermore, their geopolitical position in Rome distanced them from the influence of the lay power which resided in the capital cities of Germany, Spain, or France. This, was not the case for the Patriarchs of Constantinople and Moscow, who bore the direct brunt of any displeasure of their secular masters.

In the wake of the ecclesiastical and spiritual reforming spirit of the eleventh century, the popes, as soon as they felt reasonably secure from military repression and in control of the Church, launched an attack against the German "Holy Roman" emperors. This led to the centuries long *War of Supremacy* (1075-1313), beginning with the decisive *Investiture Controversy* of 1075-1122.

The *War of Supremacy* ended in a dialectical stalemate: the popes, while considerably reducing the power of the emperors, did not win a decisive victory. A de-facto division of power evolved at every level of society, with corresponding checks and balances on the exercise of authority. For each secular level of power there was an equivalent religious level of power: emperor/pope, king/cardinal primate, prince/bishop, small lord/parish priest.

Consequently, a *visitor* evolution developed in the peoples' minds, originating from being informed of and participating in the confrontation of the two powers, lay and religious, their ideologies and ways of life. People could reason about them, compare,them, and often play one power against the other. During this process, some of the power went to the burghers who began to look at emperors and popes, at lords and priests, with a detached and critical eye, and began to build a world free of both types of power, under the protection of a law superior to both.

That the beginning of a full-fledged *visitor ethnopsychology* occured at the time of the *Investiture Controversy* (1075-1222), had been remarked on by Colin Morris in his *The Discovery of the Individual* 1050-1200, where he wrote that: "there is a rapid rise in individualism and humanism from about 1080 to 1150" (1972, p. 7); an individualism truly unique to the West, as Morris had stressed a few pages earlier: "The Asiatic and Eastern tradition of thought has set much less store by the individual than the West has done.[16] Belief

---

[16]   Previously, when the *insular* mentality still prevailed, "The important thing was that the individual should not be left alone. The loner could do only wrong. The great sin was to stand out. Salvation lay only in and through the community; self-esteem was sin and perdition. In medieval western Europe the individual belonged first and foremost to his family. The family stifled the individual, forcing him to submit to collective ownership of property, collective responsibility, and collective action" (Le Goff, 1988, pp. 279-280).

in reincarnation virtually excludes individuality in the Western sense, for each person is but a manifestation of the life within him, which will be reborn, after his apparent death, in another form. Western individualism is therefore far from expressing the common experience of humanity. Taking a world view, one might almost regard it as an eccentricity among cultures" (p. 2).

Also Alfred Crosby, in *The Measure of Reality* (1997), remarked how, between 1250 and 1350, a marked shift from qualitative to quantitative perception occured in the West, while Carlo Cipolla, in *Before the Industrial Revolution: European Society and Economy 1000-1700* wrote: "One of the original features of Western technological development after the twelfth century was the increasing emphasis placed on the mechanical aspect of technology. There was a real passion for the mechanisation of all productive processes." (1994, p. 151)

In turn, Clifford Geertz, in *On the Nature of Anthropological Understanding,* reminded his readers that "the Western conception of the person as a bounded, unique, more or less integrated motivational and cognitive universe, a dynamic center of awareness, emotion, judgement, and action organized into a distinctive whole and set contrastively both against a social and natural background is, however incorrigible it may seem to us, a rather peculiar idea within the context of world's cultures" (1975, p. 48).

Thanks to the continuous fights between popes and emperors from 1075 to 1330, the cities gradually freed themselves from the domination of their masters. In the absence of kings and emperors the cities developed their "modern" commercial and political institutions:

> Europe's. . . . towns were marked by an unparalleled freedom. They had developed as autonomous worlds and according to their own propensities. . . . In the financial sphere, the towns organized taxation, finances, public credit, customs and excise. They invented public loans. . . . They organized industry and guilds; they invented long-distance trade, bills of exchange, the first forms of trading companies and accountancy. (Braudel, 1979, pp. 509-512)

[These towns were] to the people of Europe from the eleventh to the thirteenth centuries what America was to Europeans in the nineteenth century. The town was 'the frontier,' a new and dynamic world where people felt they could break their ties with an unpleasant past, where people hoped they would find opportunities for economic and social success, where sclerotic traditional institutions and discriminations no longer counted, and where there would be ample reward for initiative, daring, and industriousness. . . . Towns had existed in ancient Egypt, as in the classical world of Greece and Rome. In the Middle Ages, towns existed in China as well as in the Byzantine Empire. But the cities of Medieval and Renaissance Europe had something essentially different from the towns of other areas and other times. In towns of the classical world, as in the towns of China and the Byzantine Empire, the merchants, the professionals, and the craftsmen never acquired a socially prominent position. (Cipolla 1976, pp. 142-44)

Another result of the division of power between Church and State was the birth of a new and legal mentality that went far beyond the later versions of Roman law with its subservience to the emperor, and far beyond the primitive reciprocal privileges and obligations of the barbarian cultures that defeated Rome.

This new development did not only consist in written laws but in a set of ever-expanding scripts, passed down to an increasing number of individuals, from generation to generation, which made people conscious of their "rights" and created a willingness to fight for their preservation.

The contrast with other civilizations is great. In Arab countries, for instance, the caliph united in his person all religious and lay powers, which also meant full power over the legal system. Consequently, "in the Arab World, law remained an indissoluble part of religion. . . . a criminal is judged as a sinner" (Gurevich, 1985, p.155).

In China the ideal of filial relationship formed by benevolent patronage and respectful subordinationprevailed, instead of the Western notion that everybody is equal under the law:

There can be no question of anything beyond the individual's obligation to society. 'To insist on having what is supposed to be due to you is anti-social and in contravention of good manners.' In China, the norms of law did not safeguard the functioning of society and of government. . . . Hence the principle of legality, of lawful government, has no root in Chinese civilization. (ib. 1985, pp.155-56)

8. Creativity

There is no need to describe the continuous high level of creativity in the West in science, philosophy, and the arts. What must be highlighted is its high creativity, especially in the last centuries, in the most important fields of law, morality, humanitarian help, and peace. There was the abolition of slavery and torture, reduction in racial, ethnic, and gender prejudice , the foundationof the International Red Cross by Henri Dunant, in 1864, and the creation by Alfred Nobel, at the turn of the century, of five yearly prizes, one of which is for peace. Then followed, through worldwide cooperation, the creation of the League of Nations in 1919, the International Rescue Committee in 1931, the United Nations in 1945, UNICEF in 1946, the proclamation of the Universal Declaration of Human Rights in 1948, and Amnesty International in 1961.

At the root of each of these wonderful acts of creation we find the dreams and hard work of visitors shaped by several forms of division of power; DPs which gave them critical thinking within dialogue, negotiations, checks and balance; which gave them independence, self-direction, confidence; DPs which made them initiators or volunteers for the good, in an ever expanding embrace which is helping with so many problems of this world, and can do enormously more when everybody, who can, undertakes generous volunteering.

8

Triandis's Individualism vs. Collectivism Explained by Answering Hamamura's Two Questions

1. Hamamura's two questions

Takeshi Hamamura—in his 2012 article in *Personality and Social Psychology Review*, "Are Cultures Becoming Individualistic: a Cross-Temporal Comparison of Individualism-Collectivism in the United States and Japan"—asked two important questions:

1. "How is it that Western societies came to become *individualistic* and East Asian societies *collectivistic*?" p. 18[17]
2. "Perhaps the most intriguing aspect of this research is the persistence of collectivism in Japan" p. 16.

---

[17]   As explained by Triandis in *Individualism &Collectivism* of 1955 (p. 2), and quoted by Hamamura (p. 3):

> **Collectivism** *may be initially defined as a social pattern consisting of closely linked individuals who see themselves as parts of one or more collectives (family, co-workers, tribe, nation); are primarily motivated by the norms of, and duties imposed by, those collectives; are willing to give priority to the goals of these collectives over their own personal goals; and emphasize their connectedness to members of these collectives. A preliminary definition of **individualism** is a social pattern that consists of loosely linked individuals who view themselves as independent of collectives; are primarily motivated by their own preferences, needs, rights, and contracts they establish with others; give priority to their personal goals over the goals of others; and emphasize rational analysis of the advantages and disadvantages to associating with others.*

2. Answers to the First Question

A.   As discussed in the previous chapter:

Western societies became individualistic from living under Division of Power (DP): by reacting, century after century, to the intellectual demands of two major powers fighting each other: State and Church. They became individualistic by rejecting both, the Emperor and the Pope and by learning to think critically, by profiting of the war between these two powers. Western individualism evolved from the turmoil of the *War of Supremacy (1075-1313)*[18]   between the Emperor (and his claim that the Pope is nothing more than his chaplain) and the Pope (and his claim that he can dismiss the Emperor at any time[19]).

Eastern societies, instead, became and remained collectivistic under centuries of *Unity of Power* (UP).

B.   Furthermore,

Western societies became individualistic from a number of humiliations of emperors and kings—at the hand of the Church, the Communes and the Barons (in turn helped by the Church)—which contributed to endowing people with critical visitor thinking.

B1. The 1077 humiliation of King/Emperor Henry IV at Canossa

In 1077, at the invitation of Matilda, countess of Canossa, a strong supporter of the papacy in the *Investiture Controversy*, Pope Gregory stayed at the fortress of Canossa, while on his way to Germany to take action against his opponent Emperor Henry IV. To forestall his deposition, the Emperor journeyed to Canossa as a simple penitent and on January 28, after waiting for three days, received absolution. The imperial humiliation was not forgotten in Germany. For instance, Bismarck in 1872, at the height of his conflict with the Catholic Church (the so-called *Kulturkampf*), told the Reichstag his

---

[18]   Of which the *Investiture Controversy* of 1075-1122 was the first and most important episode.
[19]   Pope Gregory VII's March 1075, in *Dictatus Papae*, #12.

by-now famous *"Nach Canossa gehen wir nicht"* ("We are not going to Canossa"; indicating that he would not surrender.)

> [At Canossa] Henry gained his object, but at the sacrifice of his royal dignity. He confessed by his act of humiliation that the pope had a right to depose a king and heir of the imperial crown, and to absolve subjects from the oath of allegiance. *The head of the State acknowledged the temporal supremacy of the Church. Canossa marks the deepest humiliation of the State and the highest exaltation of the Church.* (Schaff, 1966, p. 57)

> There are few moments in history that have impressed later generations so much as this spectacle of the heir to the Empire standing in the courtyard of Canossa, a humble supplicant for papal absolution. (Brooke, 1968, pp. 69-70)

B2. The 1174 humiliation of King Henry II of England at Canterbury

> Among the earliest and most notable of these pilgrims [to the shrine of St. Thomas Becket] was Henry II himself, who came in desperation hoping to make a more lasting peace with Thomas than the reconciliation at Fréteval had been.... He proceeded to emulate the humility of his German namesake of nearly a century earlier. Subsisting on a diet of bread and water, he rode straight to Canterbury. For the last part of the journey he donned a hair shirt and the woolen shift of the pilgrim, and walked barefoot in therain from St. Dunstan's church to the cathedral.... [There] Henry submitted to flagellation from the bishops, the abbot, and each one of the eighty monks.[20] All night long he stayed in the crypt, fasting and praying. (Winston, 1967, pp. 376-7)

B3. The 1177 humiliations of Emperor Frederick Barbarossa

In 1177 the Emperor felt forced by events to renege his solemn oath of Würzburg of May 1165 never to recognize Alexander III as Pope.At Würzburg, the "Emperor himself first took the oath, then the secular princes, headed by Henry the Lion. Many of the prelates, however, avoided taking the oath or did so only with reservations. It

---

[20] "The prelates in attendance, led by Gilbert Foliot [Bishop of London] administered five strokes of the rod apiece, each of the eighty monks three strokes. As Henry survived the flagellation, it must have been largely symbolic" (Barlow, 1986, p. 270).

was decreed that a similar oath should be taken throughout the Empire within six weeks; anyone who refused was deprived of his offices, fiefs, and property... Conrad of Wittelsbach, for refusing to take the oath, was deposed from the archbishopric of Mainz..." (Jordan, 1986, p. 120). Five years later, at Fulda, Frederick solemnly repeated his intransigent declaration never to recognize Alexander (see Munz, 1969, p. 297). Then, in 1177 at Venice, in recognizing Alexander III, Frederick betrayed all those whom he had convinced or compelled to swear never to do such a thing.

There was an additional humiliation in Venice in his having to renege his pope Calixtus III, now demoted to antipope; and, at the same time, to renege his previous "imperial popes" Victor IV and Paschal III (similarly demoted), and all the cardinals and bishops who had elected and backed them.

B4. The 1215 humiliation of King John of England at Runnymede

Not only was there the humiliation of the introduction and first paragraph of *Magna Carta* discussed above, in Chapter 3 on the English, but *Magna Carta* included an insulting Article 61 indicating that the King's word was held in low regard and penalties would be imposed for breaking his word. The article provided for:

> Twenty-five barons of the kingdom who shall observe the peace and liberties we [King John] have granted, so that if we or any one of our officers, shall in anything be at fault toward anyone, or shall have broken any one of the articles of the peace or of this security, those twenty-five barons shall, together with the community of the whole land, distrain and distress us in all possible ways, namely, by seizing castles, lands, possessions....

There is nothing comparable to these four humiliations in the history of Japan or China. These two Eastern countries, for lack of a major intellectual division of power, remained *collectivistic strict ritter* (Japan), and *collectivistic insular*(China).

C. More on Japan's collectivism

Hamamura is not the first to raise his "Triandis questions." Others have asked and given answers similar to these.

C1. Eiko Ikegami's The Taming of the Samurai

In Europe, Christianity formed a powerful public institution—the post-Constantian Church—that not only claimed ultimate possession of universal truth but also wielded sufficient institutional power to compete with secular rulers. In Japan, however, no one religion was strong enough to represent an independent public power to counterbalance the state; the result was a popular tendency to use religious values as a means to achieve social and political ends....

The great difference in the relationship between religious power and secular feudal power in Europe and Japan respectively must be acknowledged.... Japanese feudalism developed without a supportive religious power comparable to the institutional strength of Christianity.... Buddhism, the dominant religion of Japan, never developed a powerful single institutional center equivalent to the Catholic Church, which claimed a monopoly of orthodox faith. In terms of ideological content, Japanese religious institutions usually did not generate a power of normative monopoly, thereby claiming superiority to the sovereign's political jurisdiction. Unlike the medieval Church, which asserted the existence of universal standards of truth and justice that were greater than the secular sovereignty of any one European country, the medieval Japanese Buddhist temples did not establish normative and transcendental values to which the secular authority should, in theory, be subject....

In order to understand the unique development of Japan's warrior culture, we must consider this relationship of Japanese feudalism with religious institutions. In Europe, the Church attempted, though not always very successfully, to transform the violence of pre-Christian warrior cultures into an ideal of Christian knighthood.... In Japan, neither the medieval nor the Tokugawa samurai had this forceful experience. There was no organized intervention by a religious-ideological power representing transcendental values that institutionally challenged samurai practices in any fundamental fashion. Even though they had the desire, the religious traditions of Japan did not have a sufficient institutional basis in most situations to enforce their values on the samurai population in general. (1955, pp. 10, 186-90)

C2. Byron Earhart's Religions of Japan (with emphasis on the fierce UP of the State)

One political factor that initially helped Catholicism gain support was the government's attempt to limit the power of Buddhist organizations (such as the monasteries on Mount Hiei): the state apparently allowed Christian missions into Japan in order to offset Buddhist strength. Eventually the government gained complete control over Buddhism and began to suspect political motives of the Catholic missionaries, all of whom came from Europe. (1984/98, p. 39)

In order to make sure that no Christians remained in Japan, the government required every family to belong to a local Buddhist temple and report all births, marriages, deaths, and changes of address to this temple. Family affiliation with a Buddhist temple became a hereditary custom: funeral and memorial rites for family members were performed by a local Buddhist temple. This set the pattern for hereditary family affiliation to local parish Buddhist temples.

It was the Tokugawa family line of military rulers that unified Japan in a form of feudal order, gaining control over the powerful Buddhist temples and then suppressing Christianity.... The Tokugawa period (1600-1867) was a time of centralization of power and stability, with foreign influence excluded. The feudal order, headed by the Tokugawa family, controlled most aspects of life and used the local Buddhist temple almost like a census office to register families.

Loyalty to superiors and to the state was stressed. Although some of these ideas originated with Confucius and later followers, they blended with Japanese notions of life and morality.*During Tokugawa times a comprehensive philosophy of life took shape in which people felt indebted for the blessings of nature and kami, expressed gratitude to parents and ancestors for the gift of life, and were loyal toward their political superiors.* (1984/98, pp. 39-40, my italics)

C3. Clayton Naff's *About Face*

Under the reign of the Tokugawas, running from the seventeenth to the nineteenth centuries, class mattered more than family. The shoguns were obsessed with keeping everyone in his place. They codified the feudal system, creating four social classes, Samurai warriors were at the top, followed by farmers, artisans, and, at the bottom of the heap, merchants.

Razan Hayashi (1583-1657), a neo-Confucian philosopher who served as adviser to the first three shoguns, recorded their views on the importance of class distinctions:

[We] cannot allow disorder between the ruler and the subject, and between those who are above and those who are below. The separation into four classes of samurai, farmers, artisans, and merchants...is part of the principles of heaven and is the Way which was taught by the Sage. (1994, p. 45)

C4. On how in the past the group was penalized for the individual who took unauthorized initiatives

The Gonin-gumi were groups of five householders who were jointly responsible for the actions of each member... The Gonin-gumi was thus an agency of self-government notarising from popular initiative but imposed upon communities by the governing class. *Its chief purpose was to preserve order and to keep the authorities informed of conditions in both town and village. It was in fact a police organ for spying and delation,* characteristic of the official attitude towards problems of administration.... Peasants were subjected to burdensome restrictions. They could not change their occupation. They could not travel outside their own district, in search of employment or to attend a wedding, until they had obtained a certificate from their parish shrine. Peasants who failed to furnish the required amount of tax goods were sometimes very harshly treated, *and it was not uncommon for thevillage headman to be deemed responsible and detained as a hostage. His property mightbe confiscated and his person subjected to torture.* (Sansom, 1963, pp. 101-05; my italics)

C5. "The [contemporary] nail that sticks up gets hammered down"

As noted by Kagawa (1997):

In Japan, those who stand out either by voicing their own opinions too directly or byexhibiting loud or showy behavior are typically rejected by the group. In other words, thenail that sticks up gets hammered down. While many Japanese understand the negativesocial climate created by this conformist way of thinking, *they also cynically understand itsimportance for survival in Japanese society.* (p. 95; my italics)

3. The answer to the Second Question

The persistence of *collectivism* in Japan is quite normal, because a collectivistic thinking from UP is the norm throughout the history of the World; and individualistic thinking from DP is rare, the result of a major *division of power* State/Church, unknown in the East.

The persistence of collectivism in Japan is also normal, given:

1. the common reproduction of cultural values, as discussed recently by Imada and Yussen in their 2012 article "Reproduction of Cultural Values: A Cross-Cultural Examination of Stories People Create and Transmit";
2. a social support associated with the motive for closeness, as discussed by Chen, Kim, Mojaverian and Morling in their 2012 article "Culture and Social Provision: Who Gives What and Why" (a comparison of Japanese with European Americans).

Yet, even without a major *division of power*, Japanese collectivism is slowly changing, given a reduction in the unity of power, and strong winds from the West:

A growing number of disillusioned Japanese are recognizing that the company claim to being a family is a sham. Tear away the facade, they say, and what you find is a feudal system. And they are right. The same martial values that reshaped the family have been imposed on men in the workplace. The martial emblems are everywhere: in the uniforms, the salutes at the entrance, the ranks of the hierarchy, and the fight-to-the-death mentality, which, I'm sorry to say, is all too literal.

Thus, whatever private feelings of independence the worker may harbor, his life, for all practical purposes, belongs to the company. Soldiers may grumble, but they may not disobey....

Half a century after General MacArthur strode into Japan, the seeds of true democracy have begun to sprout from its soil. We must acknowledge, however, that it is the Japanese people themselves who, by hard tilling, have brought them to life. In their best moments, the Japanese appear on the verge of achieving the ancient Greek ideal of democracy as freedom exercised in self-imposed moderation.

Of course, things may still go spectacularly wrong. Japanese democracy remains a frail plant in shallow soil. Economic gloom, a military threat from North Korea, or even China, or a deepening sense that America is an insatiable bully: Any of these could swiftly put Japan into a dangerous nationalistic fever. (Naff, 1994, pp. 113, 304-5)

That last statement that "Any of these could swiftly put Japan into a dangerous nationalistic fever" brings us back to the *German Proteus* of Barzini, also so often victim—and causing victims—of dangerous nationalistic fever.

9

Huizinga on the French and Netherlanders—in *The Waning of the Middle Ages*— Compared with the Italians of the Early Renaissance

1. The comparison

Huizinga noted in his seminal *The Waning of the Middle Ages: A study of the forms of life, thought and art in France and the Netherlands in the XIVth and XVth centuries* of 1924:

> We look in vain in the French literature of the beginning of the fifteenth century for the vigorous optimism which will spring up at the Renaissance[21]... Compared with current feeling in the preceding century, except in Italy, Erasmus's appreciation [for the joys of life] might rather be called warm. The men of letters at the court of Charles VII, or at that of Philip the Good, never tire of inveighing against life and the age. The note of despair and profound dejection is predominantly sounded not by ascetic monks, but by the court poets and the chroniclers—laymen, living in aristocratic circles and amid aristocratic ideas.... It is a far cry to the serene ideality of Dante's conception of noble age in Convivio! (pp. 22-26)

---

[21] Communal times, and not Renaissance—as shown later by Huizinga himself with his reference to Dante's *Convivio* of 1304-07.

But why was Italy different? As discussed in Chapter VIII, in the absence of kings and emperors, cities could develop their modern commercial and political institutions.

2. Burgundian excitability versus the communal *sang-froid* of Saint Ciappelletto of Burgundy

In the world studied by Huizinga,

> [a] general facility of emotions, of tears and spiritual up-heaval, must be borne in mind ... Solemnities of a political character also led to abundant weeping, ... documents would sometimes make us forget the vehement pathos of medieval life;... A present-day reader, studying the history of the Middle Ages based on official documents, will never sufficiently realize the extreme excitability of the medieval soul;... Every page of medieval history proves the spontaneous and passionate character of the sentiments of loyalty and devotion to the princes....The emotional character of party sentiments and of fidelity was further heightened by the powerfully suggestive effect of all the outward signs...: liveries, colours, badges, party cries. (pp. 6-14)

In Italy, it was Boccaccio who, in the very first novella of Decameron, created in Ser Ciappelletto da Prato the person least enslavedby the old scripts and emotions of the Burgundian type. And it was Boccaccio who in his second novella gave us the key to understanding Ciappelletto's great courage.

Ser Ciappelletto (after a life devoted to evil deeds, having fallen deadly sick while in Burgundy for business), in order to save the lives of the two Florentine usurers who had given him hospitality, makes a false confession to a holy friar, hoodwinks him, and, after his death, comes to be venerated as Saint Ciappelletto.

Vittore Branca called this: "cold, calculated impiety" (1976, p. 278), but impiety was only one part of the story; the other was solidarity and friendship for the two who had given him hospitality. In Ser Ciappelletto's words to them: "Do go and bring me the holiest and ablest friar you can find, if there is such a one, and leave everything to me, for I shall set your affairs and my own neatly in order, so that all will be well and you'll have nothing to complain of" (1995, p. 28).

To explain the sangfroid and courage that Boccaccio attributed to Ser Ciappelletto we simply need to read the next story: that of Abraham the Jew who had been urged by his friend Giannotto to become a Christian. However, when Abraham insisted on first making a visit to Rome, Giannotto knew that his cause was lost. Indeed, in Rome, Abraham

> cautiously began to observe the behaviour of the Pope, the cardinals, the other Church dignitaries, and all the courtiers. Being a very perceptive person, he discovered, by adding the evidence of his own eyes to information given him by others, that practically all of them from the highest to the lowest were flagrantly given to the sin of lust, not only of the natural variety, but also of the sodomitic, without the slightest display of shame or remorse, to the extent that the power of prostitutes and young men to obtain the most enormous favours was virtually unlimited. In addition to this, he clearly saw that they were all gluttons, winebibbers, and drunkards without exception.... Moreover, on closer inspection he saw that they were such a collection of rapacious money-grubbers... (ca. 1351/1995, p.39-40).

And yet, to the greatest surprise of Giannotto, Abraham decided to convert: Christianity had to be the only true religion because only a religion, sustained daily directly by the Holy Spirit, could survive and prosper with the kind of leadership he had seen at work in Rome.

Assume, now, a similar trip to Rome by Ser Ciappelletto, similar observations as those of Abraham, but a less paradoxical conclusion. In other words, assume that Ciappelletto had most naturally concluded that pope, cardinals, bishops and friars had no relations whatsoever to God, and therefore no power to absolve him of his sins past and present.

Ciappelletto may also have thought that God would approve of his saving the lives of the two hated usurers who had given him hospitality, by fooling the Burgundians who would have certainly killed them if he had died without confession, and equally killed them if he had made a true confession and—most probably—not received absolution for the extent of his sins.

In all this, it is important to remember that the *Decameron* was written in a country and times saturated with partisan propaganda which sharpened the general critical thinking: the propaganda of emperor against pope, and pope against emperor, in a country divided between papal Guelphs and imperial Ghibellines; in a country which knew very well that Dante, in his Divine Comedy, had placed three popes in Hell: Nicholas III, Boniface VIII, Clement V; in the Italy of Cecco Angiolieri (c. 1260-1312) famous for an irreverent poem which included the following verses:

> *S'i fossi papa, sare' allor giocondo*
> *che tutt'i cristiani imbrigherei;*
> *s'i fossi 'mperator, sà che farei?*
> *a tutti mozzarei lo capo a tondo.*

> If I were pope, I would be jocund
> and would cheat all Christians;
> If I were emperor, I know what I would do,
> I would chop off everybody's head.

In such a world, why should Ser Ciappelletto have had any qualms about making a false confession?

3. Who was who in Ducal Burgundy and in Communal Italy?

In the words of Huizinga:

[The Burgundian chronicler and poet Georges Chastelain (ca. 1415-75] attributes sublime virtues only to the nobility, and only inferior ones to the common people. 'Coming to the third estate, making up the kingdom as a whole, it is the estate of the good town, of merchants and of labouring men, of whom it is not becoming to give such a long exposition as of the others, because it is hardly possible to attribute great qualities to them, as they are of servile degree.' Humility, diligence, obedience to the king and docility in bowing 'voluntarily to the pleasure of the lords,' those are the qualities which bring credit to '*cestuy bas estat de François*'. (pp. 49-50)

In Italy things were different, as noted by Armando Sapori:

> The Italian merchants brought civilization everywhere and opened the way to future progress without resorting to the use of violence and warfare. They prevailed through their audacity, sustained by a subtle intuition and by high moral values: love of their country, religious faith, and culture.... Thanks to their teaching, the Italian merchant of the Middle Ages traced for individuals and peoples of all time to come the only way that leads to a full realization of humanity. (1970, p. 38)[22]

In his novellas, Boccaccio described a number of merchants "sustained by a subtle intuition and by high moral values," as the two merchants of novella I.2 (Giannotto di Civignì and Abraham Judeo), and the two merchants of novella X.3 (Mitridanes and Nathan).

Giannotto is described as "a thoroughly honest, upright man who carried a not-inconsiderable trade in cloth," and Abraham as "the soul of probity and honest dealing." The other two are paragons of hospitality and generosity: Mitridanes envies Nathan because he is more hospitable and generous than him, and decides to kill him. Unbeknownst to him, he is treated with the greatest kindness by Nathan himself who, in his total generosity, gives Mitridanes instructions on how to kill him, given that this is what Mitridanes wants. Just before killing Nathan, Mitridanes, discovers how marvelous his competitor is and repents. Ultimately, Nathan excuses his opponent with words which throw light on the anti-aristocratic views of Boccaccio and many of his compatriots:

> Nor should you feel ashamed for having wanted to kill me to acquire fame, or imagine that I marvel to hear it. In order to extend their dominions, and hence their fame, the

---

[22] Marvin Becker had similar comments: "The four centuries under review [XII to XV] were times of phenomenal growth. Individuals were able to take risks with some assurance of success. Social change transpired in a benevolent atmosphere, and it is possible to argue that the best of merchant culture could be fused with the ideals of chivalry. Of course the *Decameron* presented a world of plenty; even the plague could not diminish its generous view of human nature" (1981, p. 12).

mightiest emperors and greatest kings have practised virtually no other art than that of killing, not just one person as you intended, but countless thousands, setting whole provinces ablaze and razing whole cities to the ground. So that if, to enhance your personal fame, it was only me that you wanted to kill, there was nothing marvelous or novel about what you were doing, which on the contrary was very commonplace. (-/1995, p. 716).

4.   UP Ceremonial and Etiquette: Byzantium, the Roi Soleil, Burgundy

In the words of Huizinga:

The need of high culture found its most direct expression in all that constitute ceremonial and etiquette... Byzantinism is nothing but the expression of the same tendency, and to realize that it survived the Middle Ages, it is sufficient to remember the Roi Soleil. The court was pre-eminently the field where this aestheticism flourished. Nowhere did it attain to greater development than at the court of the dukes of Burgundy, which was more pompous and better arranged than that of the kings of France. It is well known how much importance the dukes attached to the magnificence of their household. A splendid court could, better than anything else, convince rivals of the high rank the dukes claimed to occupy among the princes of Europe. (p. 31)

Very appropriately, Huizinga compares Burgundy to Byzantium, and the Burgundian dukes to the Roi Soleil, i.e. two epitomes of the *unity of power*, of centralization, and of distance from and oppression of the people! All four—Burgundy, Byzantium, Louis XIV, and Napoleon—managed to transform so many independent minds into courtiers, so loved by Count Castiglione and by King Francis I.[23]

---

[23]   The courtiers of Francis I were despised and cursed by the jester hunchback Triboulet (Rigoletto) in Victor Hugo's *Le Roi s'amuse*, Act III: "Courtisans! courtisans! race damnée! ("Cortigiani, vil razza dannata", in Verdi's *Rigoletto*)."

5. A word from the Prince

Chastelain still calls the rich burghers villeins. He has not the slightest notion of middle-class honour.... Despoiled by war, exploited by the officials, the people lived in great distress.... They suffer in patience. 'The prince knows nothing of this.' If, at times, they murmur, 'poor sheep, poor foolish people,' a word from the prince will suffice to appease them (Huizinga, pp 50-1).

These last comments sound familiar to the students of the *unity of power*. For instance, "Napoleon was aware that 'Bravery cannot be bought with money' and deliberately aimed to create the illusion of *La Gloire* by playing on the vanity and underlying credulity of his men.... He would wander round their campfires, using his encyclopedic memory for faces to pick out here and there a veteran. 'You were with me in Egypt. How many campaigns? How many wounds?' The men loved him for his apparent interest in their records and care for their well-being" (Chandler, 1966, pp. 155-6).

6. Squashed urban pride and initiative of the Netherlanders

"Of all the Flemish cities, Ghent posed the greatest challenge to the Burgundian court. It was a textile and trade city in the hands of a political alliance of old and new wealth" (Arnade, 1991, p. 74). Ghent's unwillingness to submit to the many heavy pretensions of the Burgundian dukes led to a bloody war, in 1451-53, in which Ghent was crushingly defeated. Part of the punishment, meted out by Duke Philip the Good, included the public humiliation of the Ghentenaars when he visited the city on July 30, 1453: He forced "all the town's prominent leaders to kneel bareheaded, like common criminals, before him outside Ghent's walls. The victorious duke also forced the guildsmen to surrender their banners—now symbols of illegitimate activity" (ib., p. 76).

In 1469, from Philip's son, Charles the Bold, avenged himself on the Ghentenaars, over the troubles they had brought to his entry ceremony a year and a half earlier, when they had demanded a return to the rights they had enjoyed before their defeat of 1453.The Ghentenaars knew that they had no choice but to accept utter humiliations. After they had seen how Charles had destroyed their colleague, the city of Liège:

Ghent's aldermen, fifty-three of its guild deans and some lesser jurors all gathered [on January 8] outside the court in Brussels on the Coudenberg square, forced to wait in the snow for over one hour and a half. Chronicler Olivier de La Marche and Pierre Bladelin, *maitres d'hôtel* for the Burgundian court, finally arrived to meet the Ghent delegation. They led the wet and cold Ghentenaars inside the court central hall, now packed with prominent officials and over seventeen foreign ambassadors, and decorated lavishly with fine tapestries of classical rulers. Each guild dean carried and unfurled guild banners as he approached the central hall with other city officials. All Ghentenaars knelt thrice before entering, and carefully laid down their banners, crying 'mercy,' in unison, much like they had done after the Ghent War of 1453.

Entering the great hall, the humbled Ghentenaars saw Charles the Bold seated on an elevated throne magnificently covered with golden cloth. Charles immediately ordered his senior chancellor Pierre de Goux to shred Ghent's privilege of 1301, the bedrock of the city's right to self-governance, thereby annulling it forever before the full court....In the wake of this second humiliation ceremony, Ghent lost all claims to political autonomy. Its patricians and guild elites were forced to witness the physical and symbolic laceration of their legal privilege that granted them power in a ceremony designed to etch indelibly in their minds the price of failing to prevent unrest. (ib., pp. 91-92)

In his address to the vanquished Ghentenaars, Charles had firmly demanded that they should now behave as "good children" (ib., p. 92), the characteristic that he, and the previous dukes, had striven to develop in their subjects, and, sadly, had achieved with a good measure of success.

7. *UP* Burgundian credulity and lack of critical spirit versus Italian *DP* clever finesse

For Huizinga,

The mentality of the declining Middle Ages often seems to us to display an incredible superficiality and feebleness.

The complexity of things is ignored by it in a truly astounding manner. It proceeds to generalizations unhesitatingly on the strength of a single instance. Inexactitude, credulity, levity, inconsistency, are common features of medieval reasoning.... The credulity and the lack of critical spirit are too general and too well known to make it necessary to cite examples. (pp. 214, 216)

Instead, when we move to the world of the Italian merchants of the Middle Ages, as described by Armando Sapori, and by Boccaccio, we discover a different world. Italians of the Middle Ages did not suffer of inexactitude, credulity, levity, or lack of critical thinking. Their ships "were sailed by men for whom the voyages were not simply military enterprises or commercial ventures, but the opportunity, eagerly sought after, to know other men and other political situations, other institutions, and other mentalities, let us even say to participate in the scientific thought, spontaneous or reflective, of the cultures they touched on" (Sapori, 1970. p. 67).

Sapori also discussed an ecumenical aspect of these merchants—confirming that Boccaccio was not out of touch on the friendly relations between the Christian Torello and the Mohammedan Saladin: "Here and there, a sense of business survived in the face of the martial spirit, and this was regarded as a sign of irresponsibility by the prejudiced. When they met each other during the truces, Italians and Mohammedans violated the precepts of their respective religions, a sign of a lack of principles, but also a proof of vitality. Because of this, the contacts and collisions that put these two people in the presence of each other were not as sterile as the consequences of warfare alone would have been" (ib., p. 71).

But probably the most fascinating story, totally un-Burgundian, is Boccacio's feminist novella VI.8 (1351/1998 p. 397) in which "Caught with her lover by her husband, a lady called Philippa is summoned to judgement, and deflects its course [being burnt at the stake] with a clever defence":

In her defense, Philippa said to the Mayor of Prato:

But, as I am sure you recognize, the laws ought to be even-handed in their application, and framed with the approval of those whom they affect. This has not been the cased with this law: it threatens only us poor women—and we are far better able to satisfy several men than they are to satisfy several women. Furthermore, when this law was enactèd not a single woman consented to it—indeed not a single woman was even consulted about it. Hence this law may fairly be characterized as iniquitous" (ib., p. 399).

Could any writer under a Duke of Burgundy write anything like this? Could such a character as Lady Philippa be imagined in the *UP* world studied by Huizinga? The answer is no, but one which in no way reduces our admiration for Huizinga for having discussed a national character very common in the past, and not rare even nowadays.

8.   More *visitor* than Lady Philippa and Ser Ciappelletto: Mondino de Luzzi

The use of dissection (autopsy) of dead human bodies for scientific purposes is what differentiated Western medicine from the healing and curing approaches of the other civilizations. Because of this fundamental difference, the practice of dissection of humans deserves to be seen as the real beginning of Western medicine: *"The Greatest Benefit to Mankind"* (Porter, 1997, title).

Without dissections, there is no way to know how the human body is made, how it functions, how it can be repaired and cured. The prohibition on dissection in other civilizations has been one of the primary reasons for their lack of further medical progress beyond some very promising beginnings.

The scientific study of the human body through dissection was unique to the West for a long time. The first recorded public human dissection was conducted in Bologna in 1315 by Mondino de' Luzzi, and reported in his *Anatomia Mundini* of 1316, which became the standard text on the subject.

Built on personal experience of human dissection, the Anatomia was a brief, practical guide, treating the parts of the body in the order in which they would be handled in dissection, beginningwith the abdominal cavity, the most perishable part. (ib., p. 132)

Subsequently, public dissections—revealing anatomical structures unknown to the ancients—were instituted at the Universities of Montpellier in 1377, of Catalonia Lerida in 1391, Padua in 1429, Prague in 1460, Paris in 1478, and Tübingen, 1485.

[Prior to Mondino de Luzzi's dissections} Without any of the advances in medical science which we take for granted, medieval men and women lived permanently under the shadow of pain and bereavement. This gloomy state of affairs was, indeed, seen as an unavoidable legacy from their first parents, Adam and Eve, whose disobedience in the garden of Eden had been punished by death and suffering. Added to that was the burden of personal sin, carried by each and every individual, which might also incur the wrath of God.

Since disease was sooften perceived as the direct consequence of sin, confession offered a powerful medicine, and must often have performed an important therapeutic function. The priest, or physician of the soul, took priority over the physician of the body at the bedside of a medieval patient, not least because he was able to offer hope of salvation.... The cult of saints also offered practical benefits to the sick, who eagerly turned to pilgrimage, prayer, shrines and relics in the hope of retaining or regaining health. (Rawcliffe, 1999, pp. 1-2)

[After public dissections were authorized] The flourishing anatomical and physiological programmes created a new confidence among investigators that everything that needed to be known could essentially be discovered by probing more deeply and ever more minutely into the flesh, its systems, tissues, cells, its DNA. (Porter, 1997, p. 7)

The DP in Western Europe, in the thirteenth and fourteenth centuries, fostered the birth of scientific medicine, i.e. of science. In turn, medicine further expanded the Division of Power, and derived visitorism, by giving people an understanding and control over their bodies, away from a welter of mysterious influences impossible to know and truly influence.

10

Conclusions

Felix qui potuit rerum cognoscere causas [24]

Happy indeed are those who are knowledgeable on several national characters and their causes, because such knowledge integrates so much that is vital and fascinating about ourselves, our relatives and friends, history, religion, economics, literature, arts, and psychology.

Moving from knowledge per se, to the scholars who contributed so much to its growth, I warmly join Madariaga in his final comments, and extend them to García, Tocqueville, Bennassar, Barzini, Huizinga and Triandis and to the present book:

> Though written through the sheer fascination of the subject itself, and with a detachment which he fancies not unworthy of science, the author hopes that this essay may contribute in its small way to better international relations by strengthening the feeling of relativity in matters of national psychology. When we realize that we are all more or less the same, we are morelikely to agree. (ib., p. xvii)

And yet, that "we are all more or less the same" is wrong: *individualists* are not *collectivists*, *visitors* are not *insulars*. Takeshi Hamamura's two questions, at the beginning of chapter 8, are not rhetorical, but a cry from the heart of a scholar who would have preferred that Westerners would ask why they are not like Easterners, and why the West persists in this difference.

---

[24]   Happy the person who could know the causes of things.

The answer, therefore, must go beyond the "we are more or less the same", and search for a superior unifier, one which makes us the same (yet still historically and culturally different) in having as goal *justice, fairness and generosity*: a goal demanding thoughts and actions which not only improve daily life, but the personal and national character.

11

The Eight Scholars

1. Carlos García, Aragonese physician who arrived in Paris between 1610 and 1614: the author of the 1617 *La oposición y conjunción del los dos grandes luminares de tierra o de la antipatía natural de franceses y españoles* (Contrasts and comparisons between the two great lights of the world or the natural aversion between Frenchmen and Spaniards.

2. Alexis de Tocqueville, born in Paris in 1805, political scientist, historian and politician, author of *Democracy in America* of 1835-40.

3. Johan Huizinga, born in Groningen, Netherlands, in 1872, historian, author of *The Waning of the Middle Ages* of 1919.

4. Salvador de Madariaga, born in La Coruña, Spain in 1886, diplomat, writer, historian, author of *Englishmen, Frenchmen, Spaniards* of 1928, and *Guia del lector del Quijote* (Guide of the reader of Don Quixote) of 1926.

5. Luigi Barzini, Jr,. born in Rome, in 1908, journalist, writer, politician, author of *The Italians* of 1964, and *The Europeans* of 1983.

6. Harry C. Triandis, raised in Greece, psychologist, Ph.D. from Cornell University in 1958, author of *Culture and Social Behavior* of 1994 and *Individualism & Collectivism* of 1995.

7. Bartolomé Bennassar, born in Nîmes, France, in 1928, historian, author of *The Spanish Character* of 1975.

8. William A. Therivel, born in Paris in 1928, psychologist, author of the six-volume *The GAM/DP Theory of Personality and Creativity* of 2001-8 and *High Creativity Unmasked* of 2010.

References

Acton, John E., Lord (1862/1972). Nationality. In Lord Acton's *Essays on freedom and power* (pp. 141-170). Gloucester, MA: Peter Smith.

Amelung, Peter (1964). *Das Bild des Deutschen in der Literatur der italienischen Renaissance*. München: Max Huebner.

Anonymous (1554/1982). *La vida de Lazarillo de Tormes: De sus fortunas y adversidades*. Madrid: Clásicos Castalia.

Arnade, Peter J. (1991). Secular charisma, sacred power: Rites of rebellion in the Ghent entry of 1467. *Handelingen der Maatschappij voor Geschiedenis en Oudheikunde te Gent* (pp. 69-94).

Barlow, Frank (1986). *Thomas Becket*. Berkeley: University of California Press.

Barzini, Luigi (1965). *The Italians*. New York: Atheneum.

Becker, Marvin B. (1981). *Medieval Italy: Constraints and creativity.* Bloomington: Indiana University Press.

Bennassar, Bartolomé (1979). *The Spanish character*. Berkeley: University of California Press.

Berlin, Isaiah (1991). *The crooked timber of humanity: Chapters in the history of ideas*. New York: Alfred A. Knopf.

Boccaccio, Giovanni (ca. 1351/1995). *The Decameron*. London: Penguin.

Boccaccio, Giovanni (1351/1998). *The Decameron*. Oxford: Oxford University Press.

Branca, Vittore (1976). *Boccaccio: The man and his works*. New York: New York University Press.

Braudel, Fernand (1979). *The structure of everyday life—Civilization and capitalism 15th-18th Century, Vol. 1*. New York: Harper & Row.

Brooke, Z. N. (1968). Gregory VII and the first contest between Empire and Papacy. In J. R. Tanner, C. W. Prévite-Orton, & Z. N. Brooke (Eds.), *The Cambridge Medieval History, Volume V, Contest of Empire and Papacy.* Cambridge: Cambridge University Press.

Cantor, Norman (1993). *The civilization of the Middle Ages*. New York: HarperCollins.

Castiglione, Baldesar (1507-1516/1976). *The book of the courtier*. London: Penguin

Chandler, David G. (1966). *The campaigns of Napoleon*. New York: Macmillan.

Cheetham, Nicolas (1982). *A history of the popes*. New York: Dorset.

Chen, Jacqueline M.; Kim, Heejung S.; Mojaverian, Taraneh, & Morling Beth. Culture and social provision: Who gives what and why. *Personality and Social Psychology Bulletin, 38* (1), 3-13.

Cipolla, Carlo M. (1976). *Before the Industrial Revolution: European society and economy, 1000-1700*. New York: W.W. Norton.

Crosby, Alfred W. (1997). *The measure of reality: Quantification and Western society 1250-1600*. Cambridge: Cambridge University Press.

Csikszentmihalyi, Mihali (1988a). Society, culture, and person: a system view of creativity. In R.J. Sternberg (Ed.) *The nature of creativity* (pp. 325-39). New York: Cambridge University Press.

Dalton, O. M. (1927). *Introduction to the "History of the Franks" by Gregory of Tours*. Oxford: Oxford University Press.

Defourneaux, Marcelin (1966/1979). *Daily life in Spain in the Golden Age*. Stanford, CA: Stanford University Press.

Deutsche Heldensagen (1937). Severin Rüttgers (Ed.). Leipzig: Insel Verlag.

Diaz-Guerrero, Rogelio (1967/1975). Psychology of the Mexican: Culture and personality. Austin: University of Texas Press.

Diaz-Guerrero, Rogelio, & Diaz-Loving, Rolando (1990). Interpretation in cross-cultural personality assessment. In C.R. Reynolds & R.W. Kamphous (Eds.), *Handbook of psychological and educational assessment of children: Personality behavior, and context* (pp. 491-523). New York: Guilford Press.

Diaz-Playa, Fernando (1967). *The Spaniards and the seven deadly sins*. New York: Charles Scribner's Sons.

Dickson, H.R.P. (1951). *The Arabs of the desert: A glimpse into Badawin life in Kuwait and Sau'di Arabia*. London: George Allen & Unwin.

Drinkwater, J. F. (1983). *Roman Gaul: The three provinces*, 58 BC-AD 260. Ithaca, NY: Cornell University Press.

Earhart, H. Byron (1984/1998). *Religions of Japan*. Prospect Heights, IL: Waveland Press.

Fest, Joachim (1974). *Hitler*. New York: Harcourt, Brace, Jovanovich.

Fricke, Gerhard (1951). *Geschichte der deutschen Dichtung*. Basel: Benno Schwabe.

Funck-Brentano, Frantz (1925). *Les origines*. Paris: Hachette.

García Cárcel, Ricardo (1992). *La leyenda negra: Historia y opinion.* Madrid: Alianza Editorial.

Garcia, Carlo (1616/1992). "La oposición y conjunction de las dos grandes luminares de la tierra e de la antipatía natural de franceses e españoles." In R. Garcia Carcél *Le Leyenda Negra: Historia y opinion* (pp. 55-60). Madrid: Alianza Editorial.

Geary, Patrick J. (1988). *Before France and Germany: The creation and transformation of the Merovingian world.* New York: Oxford University Press.

Geertz, Clifford (1975). On the nature of anthropological understanding. *American Scientist, 63,* 47-53.

Geyl, Pieter (1949). *Napoleon: For and against.* New Haven, CT: Yale University Press.

Gramont, Sanche de (1969). *The French: portrait of a people.* New York: G. P. Putnam's Sons.

Gurevich, A. J. (1985). *Categories of medieval culture.* London: Routledge & Kegan Paul.

Hamady, Sania (1960). *Temperament and character of the Arabs.* New York: Twayne.

Hale, John (1994). *The civilization of Europe in the Renaissance.* New York: Atheneum.

Hamamura, Takeshi (2012). Are cultures becoming individualistic: A cross-temporal comparison of individualism-collectivism in the United States and Japan. *Personality and Social Psychology Review, 16* (1), 3-24.

Hanke, Lewis (1951). *Bartolomé de las Casas: An interpretation of his life and writings.* The Hague: Martinus Nijhoff.

Harwood, Robin L., & Lucca Irizarry, Nydia (1992). Anglo and Puerto Rican mothers' perception of attachment: Preliminary findings from the island. *Revista Puertorriqueñade Psicología, 8,* 209-26.

Harwood, Robin L., & Miller, Joan G. (1991). Perceptions of attachment: A comparison of Anglo and Puerto Rican mothers. *Merrill-Palmer Quarterly, 37,* 583-99.

Hollingdale, R. J. (1970). Introduction. In *Schopenhauer: Essays and aphorism* (pp. 9-38). London: Penguins Books.

Huizinga, Johan (1924). *The waning of the Middle Ages: A study of the forms of life, thought and art in France and the Netherlands in the XIVth and XVth centuries.* London: Edward Arnold.

Ikegami, Eiko (1995). *The taming of the Samurai.* Cambridge, MA: Harvard University Press.

Imada, Toshie, & Yussen, Steven R. Reproduction of Cultural Values: A Cross-Cultural Examination of Stories People Create and Transmit. *Personality and Social Psychology Bulletin*, 38(1), 114-28.

Irving, David (1977). *The trail of the fox: the life of Field-Marshall Erwin Rommel*. London: Weidenfeld and Nicolson.

James, Thomas Garnet H. (1978). History of Egypt to the end of the 17th dynasty. In *Encyclopaedia Britannica* (6, pp. 460-71). Chicago: Encyclopaedia Britannica.

Jordan, Karl (1986). *Henry the Lion: A biography*. Oxford: Clarendon.

Kagawa, Hiroshi (1997). *The inscrutable Japanese*. Tokyo: Kodansha International.

Kant, Immanuel (1784/1963). Idea for a universal history from a cosmopolitan point of view. In L. W. Beck (Ed.), *On history: Immanuel Kant* (pp. 11-26). New York: Bobbs-Merril.

Keen, Benjamin (1979). Preface. In B. Bennassar's *The Spanish character*. (pp. ix-xiii). Berkeley: University of California Press.

Keene, Donald (1971). Introduction. In *Chushingura: The treasury of loyal retainers* (pp. 1—26).New York: Columbia University Press.

Kleinman, Arthur, & Kleinman, Joan (1991). Suffering and its professional transformation: Toward an ethnography of interpersonal experience. *Culture, Medicine and Psychiatry*, 15, 275-301.

Lafontaine, Jean de (1668/1850). "Le corbeau et le renard." In *Fable*s, pp. 36-7. Paris: P. — C. Lehuby.

Le Goff, Jacques (1988). *Medieval civilization 400—1500*. Oxford: Basil Blackwell.

López-Ibor, Juan José (1969). *El Español y sus complejo de inferioridad*. Madrid: Rialp.

Machiavelli, Niccolò (1512/1966). Ritratto delle cose della Magna. In E. Raimondi (Ed.), *Opere di Niccolò Machiavelli* (pp. 819-25). Milan: Ugo Mursia.

Madariaga, Salvador de (1928/1969). *Englishmen, Frenchmen, Spaniards*. New York: Hill and Wang.

Marías, Julián (1941/1967). *History of philosophy*. New York: Dover.

Mann, Thomas (1939/1990). *Lotte in Weimar: The beloved return*s. Berkeley: University of California Press.

Mann, Thomas (1958). *Confessions of Felix Krull confidence man*. London: Penguin.

Maurois, André (1964). *Napoléon*. Paris: Hachette.

Menéndez-Pidal, Ramon (1946/1966). *The Spaniards in their history.* New York: W.W.Norton.

Morris, Colin (1972). *The discovery of the individual: 1050-1200.* New York: Harper & Row.

Munz, Peter (1969). *Frederick Barbarossa: A study in medieval policy.* Ithaca, NY: Cornell University Press.

Murat, I. (1984). *Colbert.* Charlottesville: University Press of Virginia.

Naff, Clayton (1994). *About face: How I stumbled onto Japan's social revolution.* New York: Kodansha International.

Nibelungenlied (Das): mittelhochdeutscher Text und Übertragung (1970). H. Brackert (Ed.). Frankfurt/M.: Fischer.

Ortega y Gasset, José (1927). *Espíritu de la letra.* Madrid: Ediciones de la Revista de Occidente.

Padfield, Peter (1984). *Dönitz: The last Führer: Portrait of a Nazi war leader.* New York: Harper & Row.

Painter, Sidney (1961). *Feudalism and liberty.* Baltimore: Johns Hopkins Press.

Patai, Raphael (1983). *The Arab mind.* New York: Charles Scribner's Sons.

Pax Facta per Dominum Fredericum Imperatorem in Civitate Constancie cum Lombardis (1183/1976). In G. D'Ilario, E. Giannazza, & A Marinoni, (Eds.), *Legnano e la battaglia* (pp. 22-35). Legnano: Banca di Legnano-Edizioni d'Arte.

Paz, Octavio (1950/1985). *The labyrinth of solitude.* New York: Grove Press.

Peyrefitte, Alain (1981). *The trouble with France.* New York: Alfred A. Knopf.

Porter, Roy (1997). *The greatest benefit to mankind: A medical history of humanity.* New York: W. W. Norton.

Porter, Roy (2001). *Enlightenment: Britain and the creation of the modern world.* London: Penguin.

Price-Jones, David (1989). *The closed circle: An interpretation of the Arabs.* New York: Harper & Row.

Rawcliffe, Carole (1999, August 9). [Medieval medicine] *Medicine for the soul.* Plenary lecture University of Cambridge.

Reischauer, Edwin O. (1977). *The Japanese.* Cambridge, MA: Harvard University Press.

Rheinstein, Max, & Glendon, Mary Ann (1993). Comparison of civil law and common law. In *Encyclopaedia Britannica*, (22, pp. 920-21). Chicago: Encyclopaedia Britannica.

Rojas, Fernando de (1499/1992). *La Celestina.* Madrid: Catedra.

Saint-Simon, Duc (1694-1723/1990). *The age of magnificence: The memoirs of the Duc de Saint-Simon.* (T. Morgan, Ed.). New York: Paragon House.

Sakae, Shioa (1956). *Chushingura: An exposition.* Tokyo: Hokuseido.

Sánchez-Albornoz (1956/1991). *España: Un enigma historico.* Barcelona: Edhasa.

Sansom, George (1963). *A history of Japan 1615-1867.* Stanford, CA: Stanford University Press.

Sapori, Armando (1970). *The Italian merchant.* New York: W. W. Norton.

Schaff, Philip (1966). *History of the Christian Church.* Grand Rapids, MI: Eerdmans.

Schiller, Friedrich (1795-99/1900). *Poems.* New York: Merrill & Baker.

Schopenhauer, Arthur (1851/1970). *Essays and Aphorisms.* London: Penguin Books.

Shirer, William L. (1960). *The rise and fall of the Third Reich.* New York: Simon and Schuster.

Smith, Bradley F. (1971). *Heinrich Himmler: A Nazi in the making, 1900—1926.* Stanford, CA: Hoover Institution Press

Staël, Madame, the Baroness de Staël-Holstein (1810/1887). *Germany.* Boston: Houghton, Mifflin and Company.

Tocqueville, Alexis de (1834-40/1987). *Democracy in America, Volume II.* New York: Alfred A.Knopf.

Tocqueville, Alexis de (1834-40/1988). *Democracy in America.* New York: Harper Perennial.

Triandis, Harry C. (1994). *Culture and social behavior.* New York: McGraw-Hill.

Triandis, Harry C. (1995). *Individualism & collectivism.* Boulder, CO: Westview.

Unamuno, Miguel de (1906/1951). "Sobre la Europeización". In *Ensayos (1,* pp. 901-20). Madrid: Aguilar.

Vaillé, Eugène (1950). *Le Cabinet Noir.* Paris: Presse Universitaire de France.

Vatikiotis, P. J. (1987). *Islam and the state.* London: Croom Helm.

Wallace-Hadril, J. M. (1957). Frankish Gaul. In J. M. Wallace-Hadrill & J. McManners (Eds.), *France: Government and society.* (pp. 36-60). London: Methuen.

Weiten, Wayne (1989). *Psychology: Themes and variations.* Pacific Crove, CA: Brooks/Cole.

Wiley, W. L. (1967). *The formal French*. Cambridge, MA: Harvard University Press.

Winston, Richard (1967). *Thomas Becket.* New York: Alfred A. Knopf.

Yiannopoulos, Athanassios N. (1973). Code Napoléon. In *Encyclopaedia Britannica (6*, pp. 10-11). Chicago: Encyclopaedia Britannica.

Author Index

Subject Index